D0236504

The Toilet Book

Also by Bill Oddie

Bill Oddie's Little Black Bird Book
Bill Oddie's Gone Birding

The Toilet Book

Bill Oddie & Laura Beaumont

Methuen

First published in Great Britain 1984
by Methuen London Ltd
11 New Fetter Lane, London EC4P 4EE

Design by Christopher Holgate

Printed in Great Britain by
Richard Clay (The Chaucer Press) Ltd.,
Bungay, Suffolk

British Library Cataloguing in Publication data:

Oddie, Bill
The Toilet Book.
I. Title II. Beaumont, Laura
828'.91409 PN6175

ISBN 0-413-56910-1

WHERE TO PUT IT

This Book is intended to be kept and read — IN THE TOILET —

This doesn't of course mean that you can't read it before you go or indeed after you've been. In fact you can – and *should* – read it anywhere where a 'visit' may be imminent. When travelling you should always carry a copy; you would also be well advised to keep another by your bedside; there should always be one on your coffee table, so that guests may read it; and no toilet in your home should be without it. If there are any of your friends that don't have one, you would be doing them a great favour by buying it for them immediately.

About twenty-five copies should cover everything.

WHAT'S IN IT

If you are an average healthy person you spend 11½ minutes per day going to the toilet. That is 1 hour 20 minutes and 30 seconds per week – well over a quarter of a day each month – nearly half a week every year or – several MONTHS of YOUR lifetime – TOTALLY WASTED! This need not be so. Now, THIS book teaches you how you can learn exciting and useful skills, acquire fascinating new knowledge and achieve GREATER FULFILMENT whilst you are in your toilet.

Of course it is possible to concentrate and learn only when one is feeling relaxed and confident. In the privacy and comfort of your own toilet, in your own home, conditions should be ideal. Unfortunately, when you are forced to visit other people's toilets you may not find the atmosphere quite so conducive. No lock on the door, no paper, a faulty cistern, unwanted and uncontrollable noises – all these undermine your enjoyment of what should be an opportunity for enlightenment, not a journey of embarrassment. The toilet should be a temple of knowledge, not of fear. Therefore this book is divided into TWO PARTS.

PART ONE deals with self-improvement, whilst PART TWO deals with emergencies. It surely goes without saying that if you are experiencing an emergency at this very moment you should stop reading this introduction at once and turn immediately TO PART TWO.

If, however, you are sitting comfortably, but with nothing more to occupy you than fulfilling the natural functions you came in for, then read on and look forward to PART ONE, wherein you will discover a wealth of fascinating activities you can enjoy RIGHT NOW without in any way impeding or interrupting the essential business of toilet-going.

HOW TO USE IT

If you intend to revisit this loo frequently (which presumably you will if it's your own) then take your time. Read these introductory passages first and then work your way through at leisure, absorbing our suggestions either in written order or at random, depending on your needs, moods or inclinations at the time of each visit.

If, however, this visit is a 'once-off', or you don't expect to be back here for a while, stop reading this bit now, turn to page xiii, have a skim down the contents list, and choose something that appeals to you. We would suggest a self-contained item, and preferably not *too* interesting. If you become very absorbed you'll either be in here for far too long and, if you're out visiting, your hosts will consider this anti-social or even suspicious (they may even come looking for you!), or you'll be tempted to keep coming back during the evening, which is bound to worry your hosts even more. They'll start asking all sorts of questions about your health, which will embarrass you, and they may show concern or sympathy which you don't deserve and that'll make you feel guilty. So . . . make sure you choose an APPROPRIATE ACTIVITY for the circumstances. This will depend on several things. . . .

Consider, for example, the shape, size and layout of the toilet you are in. What is its decorative condition? What equipment does it contain? Is the floor covered in hard tiles (excellent for tap-dancing) or soft carpet (useless for tap-dancing but splendid for golf)?

Are the walls plain or hung with pictures? (This could affect its appropriateness for ball games.) Is the toilet also the bathroom? (If so, it may contain all manner of useful accoutrements – including possibly even a partner.)

And how long are you intending to be in there? Are you feeling fit and 'normal'? (If you *do* have a 'problem' you have the consolation that the longer you are in there the more you'll learn.)

Whatever you do, DON'T OVER-REACH YOURSELF – you could cause all sorts of damage to person and property. Choosing the appropriate activity (and dealing with problems) is a matter of observing, appreciating, and accepting the conditions and making the most of them. It's all part of TOILET AWARENESS. . . .

Here are plans of several typical toilet/bathroom arrangements. Study them and decide which of them is most similar to the one you are now on. In the following chapters we shall clearly indicate the appropriateness of any particular activity to the particular toilet.

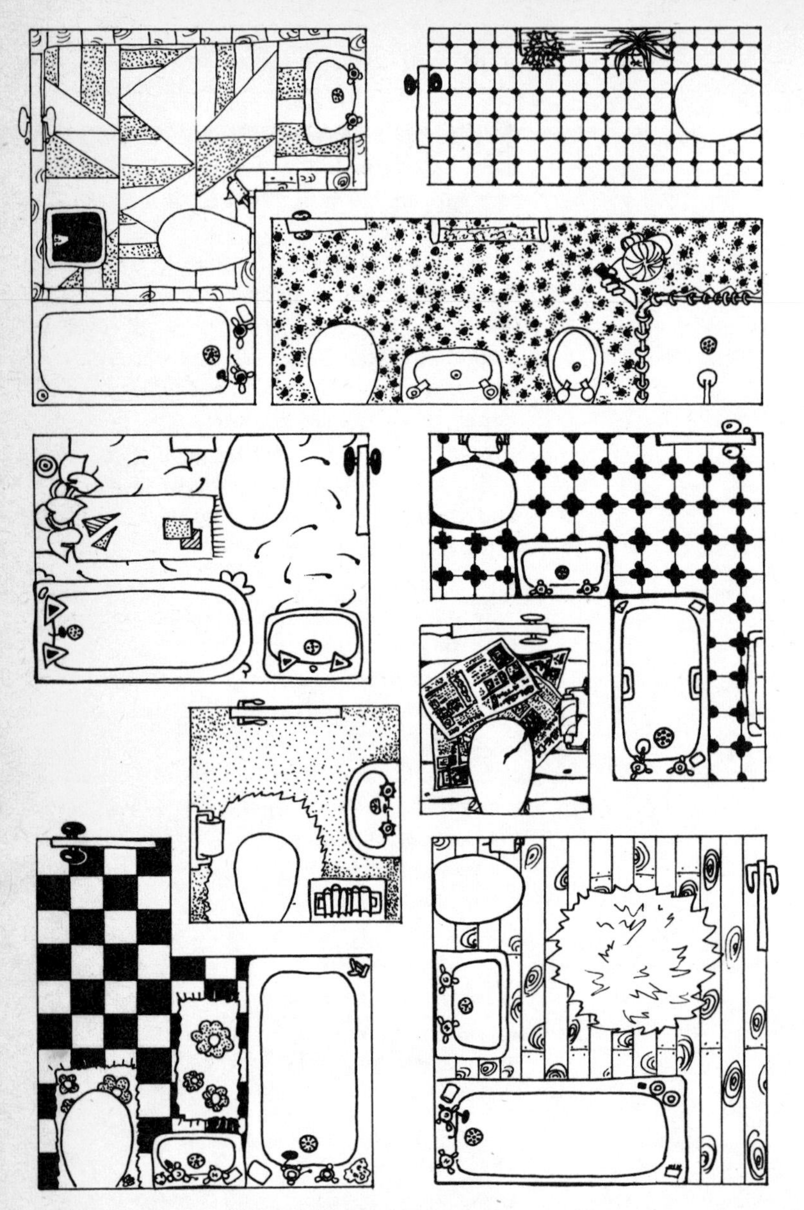

Fig. 1. If you have difficulty recognising *your* toilet from this angle, go into the room above, knock a hole through the floor, and look down. You may also like to colour this in.

EQUIPMENT

You will soon learn to equip your own loo with the gear you need to practise your 'special interests'. We would, however, suggest that the following items are more or less essential: a lock on the door; toilet paper; a toilet seat; a cistern that flushes properly; walls and a floor (a ceiling is not indispensable but is desirable); a mirror; and this book. If you find yourself in a toilet lacking any of these facilities, turn to PART TWO.

If all is well . . . here is the LIST OF CONTENTS.

List of contents

Part Two Other people's toilets

Part One

Self-improvement in the toilet

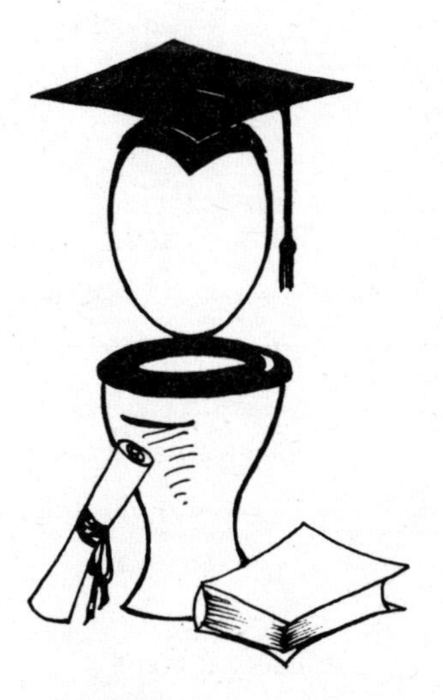

The always open university . . .

Keeping fit

How often have you said, 'Oh, I'd love to try and keep myself fit but somehow I can never find the time!'?

Well, you've found it. Eleven and a half minutes a day of sensible exercise is quite enough to keep anyone in shape. All the following movements and positions can be accomplished whilst fulfilling natural toilet functions and will in no way impede your efficiency, regularity or accuracy.

Basic gymnastic exercises

What you are capable of will depend on your 'toilet position'. Generally speaking you can do more whilst sitting (both sexes) than when standing (men only, we presume).*

MEN STANDING should restrict themselves to ARM RAISING. Hold yourself in your left hand, raise your right arm up – count 'two three' – then lower it – 'two three' – reach out sideways – 'two three' – and then reach down and CHANGE HANDS. Now, holding yourself in your right hand, repeat the movement with the left arm. Practise these exercises till you can do them very quickly indeed. Look at your watch –

* (From now on we shall be referring to the former position as 'No. 1 toilet position' and the latter as 'No. 2 toilet position'.)

carefully. How many movements can you achieve during the average time you take to relieve yourself? As you become more adept you may care to add 'neck-circling', but be sure that in taking your eye off the business in hand you don't divert your aim. Eventually you may be able to release yourself entirely and do the movements with BOTH ARMS at once, AND neck-circling at the same time; but don't attempt it in someone else's toilet till you have perfected it at home.

Whilst sitting (men and women)

There are no end to the beneficial exercises that can be practised in this position. Most of them are fairly strenuous and will not only keep you fit but will actually facilitate bowel movement.

Jogging

Simply sit there and move your legs up and down as if you are trotting through the park. (You may care to wave to imaginary passers-by to enhance the illusion.) Then increase your pace to . . .

Running on the pot

and finally to . . .

Sprinting

Making sure you get your knees up as high as possible, pummel the floor with your feet and pump with your arms. Assuming you take about three and half minutes for a complete toilet visit, you will achieve the equivalent of a world record for the 1500 metres.

Most *Gymnastic movements* are also possible, such as . . .

Touching your toes (though do make sure you don't topple forward and bump your head – beware of hard tile floors) and

Leg raising This is an ideal toilet exercise. Sit upright with back straight and pressed against the cistern. Raise your left leg to the level of the rim of the bowl . . . and lower. Raise right leg and lower. Now raise both legs . . . open them as wide as possible (make sure you have entirely removed your trousers or pants) . . . and close . . . and lower. Keep counting.

There are many variations on this theme but be sure you *never* lift your legs higher than the rim, or you may slide deeper into the bowl and get stuck. (If this does happen, turn to page 72.)

Fig. 2.

These are merely a few basic suggestions. We recommend that you attend one lesson of a keep fit class (usually given free 'on approval') and then, instead of going again and wasting all that money, adapt the exercises to the toilet. These movements will improve your strength and stamina.

To increase your suppleness have a go at *Yoga.* You will be pleasantly surprised at how many yoga positions can be achieved on the toilet without impairing your functions.

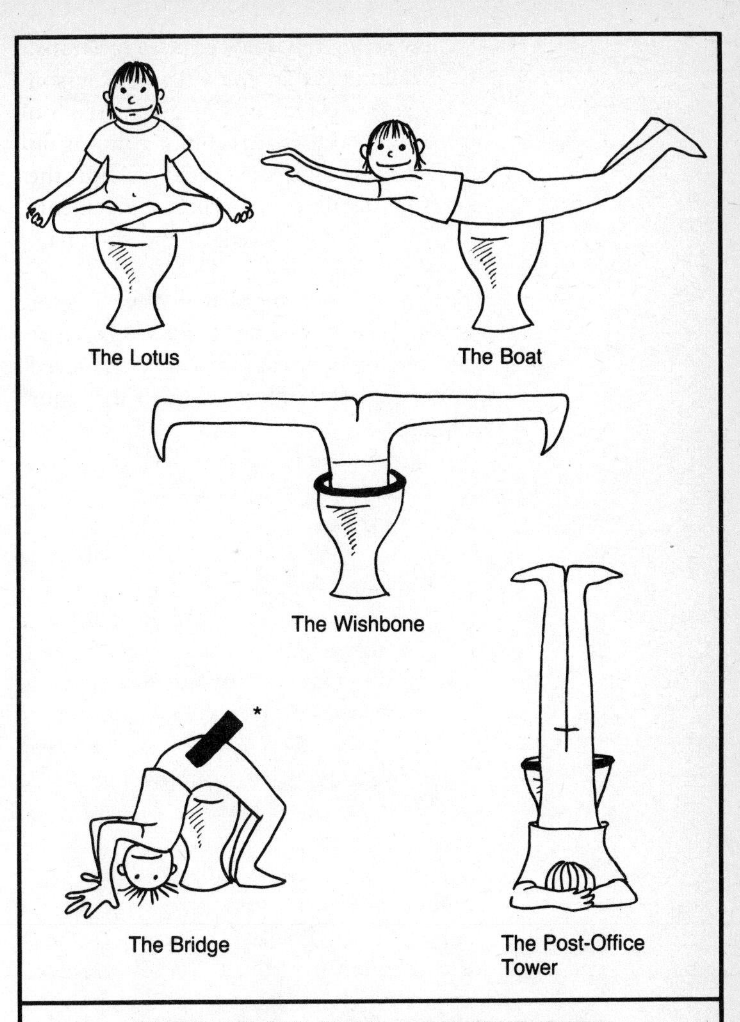

Fig. 3. **FIVE EASY YOGA POSITIONS**

Before adopting a posture remind yourself what toilet-function you came in to perform and make sure it's possible

*This is not a house brick

Sport

Once you have achieved fitness you will want to use it recreationally or competitively. There are many sports you can practise in the toilet, but you must also accept that there are an awful lot you can't. Do NOT, for example, attempt the Pole Vault, American Football, Ice Hockey, or Show-Jumping. However, you should be able to improve your . . .

Golf

A man standing in front of the toilet places his feet in what is essentially the ideal posture for teeing-off. So you may PRACTISE YOUR STANCE – but NOT YOUR SWING (unless you are quite bizarrely endowed!). There is no reason why you shouldn't keep a spare club and ball in your toilet, in which case it is the ideal place to practise your CHIP SHOTS from a SITTING POSITION.

However, this is only possible if the toilet is in a bathroom with the bath on the left (or the right, if you are left-handed), and preferably with a thick pile carpet to simulate 'the rough'. Place the ball between your feet and attempt to chip it into the plughole. You may find the club easier to manipulate in this posture if you saw a foot or two off the shaft.

With practice you should become very expert but you may find yourself so conditioned that you will only be able to achieve the shot when you are sitting down. This doesn't really matter since the next time you are out on the golf course your opponent will be greatly impressed and intimidated by your nonchalance when you set up your shooting-stick in a bunker, sit down, produce your sawn-off club, and chip straight into the hole for a birdie two!

Darts

Keep a dartboard on the inside of the toilet door (make sure the lock works) and a set of darts in the toothbrush holder (but for God's sake don't clean your teeth with them, though you could use them as toothpicks).

Ball games

Table tennis is an ideal toilet game. We don't suggest you set up a net, or take in an opponent (nor indeed a table) but you can greatly improve your reactions by sitting there and belting a ping-pong ball round the loo. It will fly back at you from the most unexpected angles but it is so light it can't do much damage. The same principle applies to improving your *Squash*. Remember though that the ball is harder, so don't try it unless there are no windows, no pictures on the walls and no glass shelves full of breakables. In both cases the ultimate test of your skill is to prevent the ball rebounding between your knees and ending up down the toilet.

Badminton is not strictly a ball game but it is perhaps

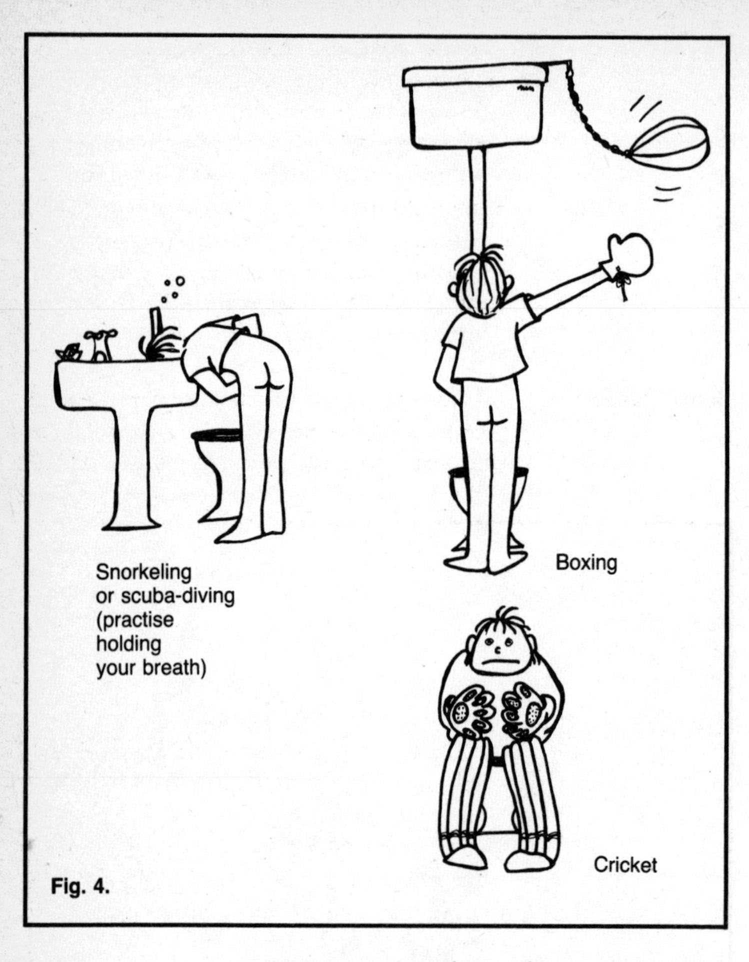

Fig. 4.

even more suited to toilet practice, especially since you may not even have to take in any special equipment. You should be able to manage with a loo brush as a racket and a cotton wool ball (or even screwed-up paper) as the shuttlecock. And don't forget

Cricket

Sitting on the loo means you are in a very

similar posture to a wicket-keeper crouching behind the stumps. So why not keep a set of wickets in your toilet, and practise whipping off the bails? Moreover, with a little ingenuity you can set up a contraption triggered by your foot which will propel a rock-hard cricket ball straight at your most sensitive and, at this time, completely unprotected area. We can think of no better incentive for learning how to catch it.

Board games

Toilet chess is a particularly exciting game. Everyone who uses your toilet has to make a move – in fact they are not allowed to

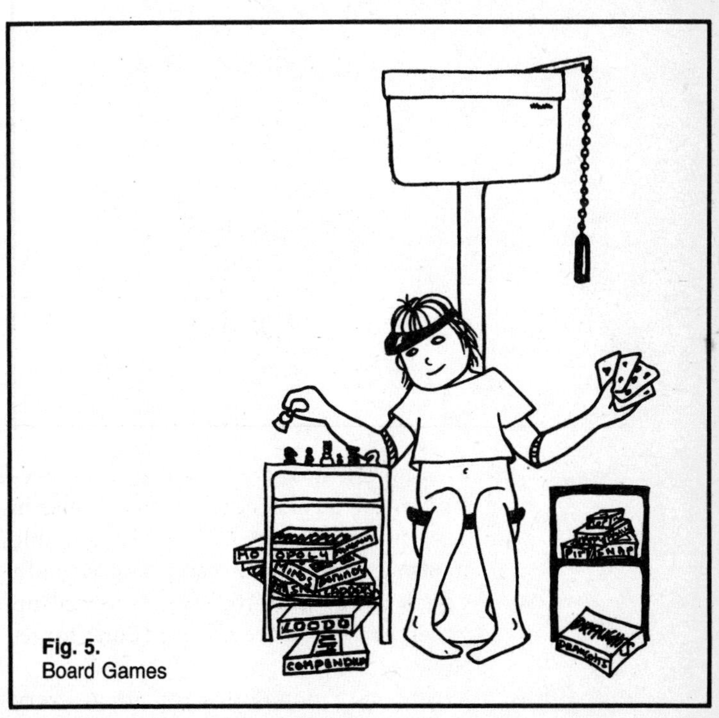

Fig. 5.
Board Games

leave until they have done so (an electronic lock may be fitted to the door that can only be released by moving a chess piece). The same principle can be applied to *Monopoly*, but be prepared for the game to go on for twenty or thirty years.

Ventriloquism

Who amongst us has not gazed in admiration at those remarkable people who have harnessed the ability to make a doll made out of wood appear to talk, sing and disappear into a suitcase?

Being able to 'throw one's voice' is possibly one of the most coveted and envied skills in modern society. To be capable of such an artistic feat would provide the user not only with a terrific power with which to alarm and mystify, but also an endless source of entertainment for others. Adults and children alike love nothing better than to watch a little man sitting on a big man's lap making smart-Alec remarks. They also enjoy a VENTRILOQUIST.

And where better to pursue that subtle and elusive art than the comfort of your smallest room?

In the following chapter we will be teaching you how to pronounce difficult letters without moving your lips, how to throw your voice, make complete fools out of your friends, and construct your own ventriloquist's dummy out of what you can see around you. All in the time you would spend daily in your WC.

Loosening Up – Facial Exercises

The first journey along the rocky road to 'ventriloquial perfection' will be a lonely one. You must learn to use your facial muscles and exercise and loosen your tongue before you can credit the sounds you are making to any other source (e.g. the VENTRILOQUIST'S DUMMY.)

The exercises are quick, easy and can be done in a No. 1 and No. 2 toilet position, by ladies or men.

Oh, by the way, it is imperative to have a mirror in there with you to check facial movement whilst exercising. You may not *think* you are moving your lips, but to a casual observer you are gibbering like a chimpanzee. So if there isn't one already in there make sure you take one in with you when you go.

(N.B. If you do feel slightly uncomfortable, for one reason or another, about the *louder* vocal exercises, you can use any of the non-vocal 'noise-covering devices' from the chapter headed 'Covering the Noise' (page 74). That's if the noises you are making aren't already covering the noises you are making . . . if you see what we mean.)

Tongue and face exercises for suppleness and strength

For best results do the whole routine once through every day.

1 Move your tongue around in a circle in front of your teeth. *Six times* clockwise then *six times* anti-clockwise.

2 Try to swallow your tongue *three times*,

then gently stick it out and pull it *three times*.

3 Poke out your tongue and touch your nose *three times*. Touch your chin *three times*. Then nose, chin, nose, chin . . . etc *six times*.

4 Put one finger in each corner of your mouth and pull gently.

5 Stretch out your lips as hard as you can in a smile, a sad face, a pout, a monkey face, a wide open scream (no sound yet!).

6 Now, stretching your face as taut as you can, shout 'Ooh! Ah! Ooh! Ah! Ooh! Ah!' *fourteen times*. Now the reverse: 'Ah! Ooh! Ah! Oooh! Ah! Ooh!' *fourteen times*.

7 (The following exercise will possibly make you hear a buzzing sound in your head.)

(Sing) 'Buz Buz Buzzzzzzzzzzzzzz zod zod zod.' If you feel slightly dizzy, it's a good sign! Continue until you fall off the toilet. Your face is now loosened up and you are now capable of true ventriloquial effects.

The Difficult Sounds Everybody knows which consonants give away a bad ventriloquist. P, B, M, V and F. Let's work up to them. Now is the time to use your mirror – watch your mouth closely.

a Grit your teeth and smile naturally

b Sing these words without moving your lips: 'Diggy diggy dong dong doo doo dah! Dilly dilly willy willy weeeee!'

(The D sound is no problem but you may

have trouble with the W. Try thinking W but saying OO so willy becomes Ooilly.)

Now try the song with every consonant of the alphabet with the exception of the ones mentioned above, always remembering to keep your 'willy willy wee' on the end. You should not find that too difficult, but now for the 'problem' ones.

P The sound P is formed by *thinking* the letter P but saying T, e.g. potty becomes 'totty'.

B The sound B is formed by *thinking* the letter B but saying VH, e.g. 'ballcock' becomes 'vhallcock'.

M The sound M is formed by *thinking* the letter M but saying NG with a little hum before it, e.g. 'mirror' becomes 'mmm . . . ngirror'.

V The sound V is formed by *thinking* the letter V but saying TH, e.g. 'Vaseline' becomes 'Thaseline'.

F The sound F is formed by *thinking* the letter F but saying H, e.g. 'flannel' becomes 'hannel'.

Now try the 'Diggy diggy dong' song with each of *these* letters.

Remember to smile . . . we don't want to see anything moving. Do you feel a vibration? It's probably someone banging on the door but don't worry, it won't be long before you can throw your voice into the corridor and tell them to go away!

After only a *few days* of practising the

above exercises you should have achieved the 'near-perfect ventriloquial voice', but the graft is not over yet! The fun is yet to come. . . .

Producing a muffled voice from inside confined space with or without lid

The WC itself is a perfect location to perfect such a feat! Once confident and competent you can wreak havoc in your household. Disembodied voices can come from anywhere and everywhere and the culprit need never be revealed!

In order to perfect the 'muffled voice' you must do the following:

a Take a deep breath
b Grit your teeth and smile
c Arch your tongue back so it is sticking down your throat. This will cause your voice to have a 'muffled' effect. It might also cause you to vomit, which is another good reason for doing it in the toilet.

Your 'near-perfect ventriloquial voice' is now coming out of your nose. Use this method when speaking in the voice of the person in the confined space – your own voice will be as normal.

NB. It's as well to give the 'muffled voice' some character, a foreign accent or speech impediment perhaps?

The Performance

No artiste can be happy practising his or her art alone. You *need* an audience. Why not try the following script?

Open the toilet door and attract the attention of a passer-by: a visiting relation maybe, or your daughter's teen-age boyfriend.

YOU (*in your voice*): Hey . . . come and listen to this . . . I thought I heard something.

(*They will then follow you into the toilet and watch as you lift the lid ever so slightly.*)

YOU (*in muffled voice*): Help! I've fallen down the toilet!

YOU (*in normal voice*): What?

YOU (*in muffled voice*): I said, I've fallen down the toilet!

(Remember: P becomes T – 'Helt!'; V becomes TH – 'I'the'; and F becomes H – 'Hallen'. Hence: 'Helt! I'the hallen down the toilet!' And *don't* hide behind the lid so they can't see your mouth moving!!!)

By this time, whoever you have dragged into the toilet will be spellbound. Either that or they will have walked out. You continue:

YOU (*in normal voice*): Well . . . what *are* we going to do?

YOU (*in muffled voice*): Throw me down a letter opener!

YOU (*in normal voice*): Throw you down a what?

YOU (*in muffled voice*): A letter opener!

YOU (*in normal voice*): A letter opener?

YOU (*in muffled voice*): Yes, a letter opener!

(Do this quickly enough and your audience may well applaud.)

YOU (*in normal voice*): Why do you need a letter opener?

YOU (*in muffled voice*): Because I'm stuck in the 'S' bend!

YOU (*in normal voice*): Well, I don't know who you are, but you're certainly very funny.

At this point you may feel you should admit the joke to the bemused onlooker as they may be so convinced they might rush from the room and call a plumber. After all, you don't want them to miss

The dummy

The above exchange is pretty self-contained and can work well as a short demonstration of your new art, but it can also herald the arrival of your home-made (or should I say 'toilet made') ventriloquist's doll – 'Lotty Loo-Brush'! Yes . . . at last the friend is nigh! and you need go no further than your WC. All you need to create Lotty is all around you! (See over.)

When we have Lotty you can continue the 'S' Bend routine from where we left off, providing your audience is still there. The 'muffled voice' now becomes Lotty, who you are carefully concealing round the back ready for her surprise arrival. (You hope the onlooker hasn't noticed the lipstick on your hands.)

YOU: Now be serious. What WILL get you out of there?

LOTTY: A bottle of bleach. (*Think B but*

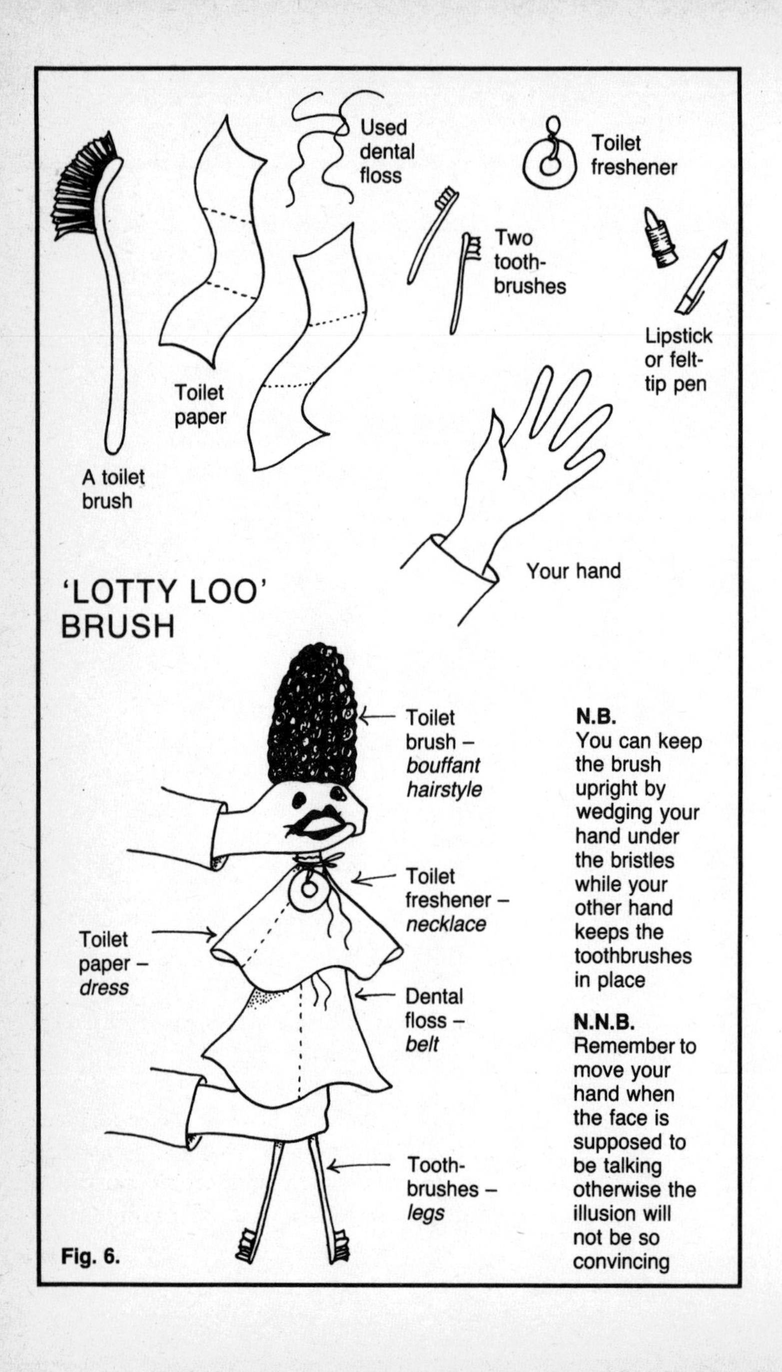
Used
dental
floss
Toilet
freshener
Two
tooth-
brushes
Lipstick
or felt-
tip pen
Toilet
paper
A toilet
brush
Your hand
'LOTTY LOO'
BRUSH
Toilet
brush –
bouffant
hairstyle
Toilet
freshener –
necklace
Toilet
paper –
dress
Dental
floss –
belt
Tooth-
brushes –
legs
N.B.
You can keep
the brush
upright by
wedging your
hand under
the bristles
while your
other hand
keeps the
toothbrushes
in place
N.N.B.
Remember to
move your
hand when
the face is
supposed to
be talking
otherwise the
illusion will
not be so
convincing
Fig. 6.

say VH – i.e. a 'vbottle of vbleach'.)

YOU: A bottle of bleach?

LOTTY: Yes, a bottle of bleach. A *big* bottle of bleach. A *big beautiful* bottle of *blue* bleach. . . .

YOU: A BIG . . . OH YOU'RE JUST PLAYING GAMES.

LOTTY: But I like games. How about a game of ball, cock!?

YOU: I've had enough of this nonsense. Come out this minute.

Now prepare yourself for Lotty's entrance. You have to give the impression you've just pulled her out of the toilet. Tussle and wrestle for a bit as if you are having a fight, and hopefully your body will cover the moment when she's produced. With any luck quite a crowd will have gathered by now to see what all the commotion is about. Turn round and show Lotty to the audience. (They will possibly gasp.)

YOU: Phew . . . what a palaver!

LOTTY: Well, you can't get me out of your cistern that easily!

YOU: You know something, Lotty?

LOTTY: Yes, William, you're daft. . . .

BOTH: As a brush! (*This could be tricky but it's worth a try.*)

Now smile and bow to the audience. Lotty should curtsey. We guarantee that not only will your audience be surprised that you have managed to acquire such skills in what appeared to be no time at all, they will walk away muttering that they have never seen anything quite like it in their lives before.

Your own toilet is possibly the best place to work when you are at the later stages of ventriloquism i.e. the act, patter, repartee etc. It is where you will keep the makings of your own familiar dummy and a well positioned mirror; although it is not impossible to practise your facial and vocal exercises in any WC you happen to find yourself in. Just remember to take a mirror in with you (or use the reflection ruses on page 88), and keep the noise level to whatever is acceptable to your credibility and your host's generosity. You can even fashion a 'makeshift' dummy to practise on. Look around for something you can make talk (gentlemen may have an advantage here).

Opposite are some useful suggestions.

These are just a few of the things you can do. We're sure that you can find many, many more. Remember, we can only start you off. It's up to you to develop and explore the avenues along the way. You may discover you have a natural talent for entertaining that could go even beyond the toilet – in which case why not turn to page 47 and become a real all-rounder. Good luck!

BAGGY
Sanitary-towel disposal bag
Paint cheeky face on bag
ROLY-POLY
Two cotton buds
Soft toilet roll
Squeeze cotton buds in roll
PLUNGO
A Plunger
Paint black dots on your fingertips
Your fingers are eyes
Fig. 7.

Improving your word power

There are many words which we hear or read fairly often that, if we are honest, we have never *really* understood. They are usually used by politicians or critics. If we don't understand a word we don't like to admit it, and so we never realise that nobody else understands it either (quite possibly including the people who are using it). If we were all honest and owned up we feel sure it would be a comfort to us all to realise there are certain words that NOBODY understands. Here are five of them:

> VOLUBLE . . . EGREGIOUS . . .
> ETHOS . . . ECLECTIC . . . and . . .
> PECCADILLO.

Now of course there may be a *few* other words you don't understand either (or hundreds, if you are a real dumdum), but we can't put them all in here otherwise this book would not be a 'toilet book', it would be a dictionary. Not that we disapprove of dictionaries – not at all, in fact we suggest that you keep one in the toilet (as well as, not instead of this book).

Spend a few visits underlining all the words you don't understand (or if you *are* a dumdum, it might be quicker to underline the ones you *do* understand). On each subsequent toilet trip try and assimilate the meaning of another five new words (starting with 'assimilate').

Meanwhile, let's get back to those five unintelligible words (we presume you know 'unintelligible'). Say them out loud and try to pronounce them correctly – you may be using them sooner than you think.

Voluble (vol-yoo-bul). Egregious (i-gree-jus). Ethos (eethos). Eclectic (i-klek-tik). Peccadillo (pek-a-dil-oh).

They sound *really* impressive, don't they?

Wouldn't you *love* to use them? Perhaps you are even now at a dinner party and have escaped into the loo because you can't think of a thing to say. Well, any minute now you are going to burst out more eloquent than Malcolm Muggeridge.

OK – here's what those words mean (and these are the real definitions, so don't go looking for funny jokes that aren't there). Say them out loud again as you learn the truth.

Voluble: Is not a game played by nudists (that's 'volley ball') nor the worth of a Ming Vase (that's 'valuable'). It is in fact an adjective meaning: 'speaking or spoken with great fluency'.

Egregious: Doesn't mean birds that like living in big flocks (that's 'gregarious'). It is in fact a peculiar-sounding adjective meaning: 'outstandingly bad'.

Ethos: No, *not* the statue in Piccadilly Circus (that's Eros) nor the fourth Musketeer (that was Athos). It is a noun meaning: 'the characteristic spirit and beliefs of a community, person or literary work'.

Eclectic: An 'eclectic' is not a member of either a religious sect or a pop group; nor is it a word that we can think of any other silly misunderstanding about. It is in fact an adjective meaning: 'choosing or accepting from different sources'.

Peccadillo: Not a small hard South American animal (that's an '*arma*-dillo') nor anything used in bullfighting (though it sounds as if it should be). It is a noun which rather disappointingly means: 'a trivial offence'.

OK. Now you're nearly ready to use your new-found word power and dazzle the waiting guests: but ... don't get over-excited. You may not have completely assimilated the proper usage of the new words (especially if you still don't know what 'assimilate' means). So, here are examples of how they should be used in context. We suggest you try and wangle the after-dinner conversation so that you can validly incorporate the following sentences. We have tried to make them appropriate so that you should be able to slip them naturally and easily into any typical light-hearted discussion of the meal, the weather, the host's children etc. ...

Voluble

On returning from the toilet to the dinner table you can say:

'Hey up folks, I bet you didn't expect me to come out of the lavvy as *voluble* as this did you?'

Egregious

On discussing the weather:

Host: 'My my, it's been dreadful weather lately, hasn't it?'

Other Guests: 'Shocking', 'Awful', 'Beastly'.

You: 'Bloody *egregious* if you ask me!'

Ethos

On realising the guests are a little shocked by your coarse language.

'Well . . . I just say the first word that comes into my head – that's my *ethos*.' (This usage may not be strictly correct but we don't understand the definition, let alone the word.)

Eclectic

On being asked whether you'd like 'Tomato, Brown, or Worcester on your chips', you reply:

'You know me – when it comes to what I put on my chips I'm totally *eclectic*.'

(If anyone else knows the word this should get quite a laugh as it is a rather clever pun. If you refer back to the definition of 'eclectic' you'll see what we mean: 'choosing from various sources'. 'Source' is pronounced the same as 'sauce' – get it? Oh, and incidentally two words pronounced the same are called 'homophones' (unless of course they're the same word said twice).

Peccadillo

When the host chastises his little boy. . . .

Host: Dear me, Tarquin, you *are* a naughty boy, you *never* eat your dinner. Look what you've left on your plate . . . half your artichoke.'

You: Oh leave off the boy, it's a mere *peccadillo*. . . .

Witty guest: No, it's an artichoke!

This allows everyone to join in the verbal fun started by the 'eclectic' joke. Probably. On the other hand. . . .

Don't be surprised if the other guests look bored and bemused. This is because, of course, they have no idea what any of those words mean (though they will have once they too have been to the toilet).

Now we dare say there will be some clever-dick-smarty-pant-show-offs reading this who *knew* what those five words meant all along. OK then, check this lot out. Do you *honestly* and *truly* know the meaning of:

Anomaly. Autonomous. Acronym. Aegis. Adjure. Arcane. Atavistic. Brackish. Calumny. Colloquy. Contumely. Crepuscular. Deleterious. Detritus. Exiguous. Extirpate. Extrude. Fecund. Foment. Febrile. Genuflect. Hermetic. Internecine. Invidious. Insouciant. Logistics. Meretricious. Munificent. Mendacious. Nefarious. Oxymoron. Opprobrium. Plangent. Pachyderm. Palindrome. Peremptory. Persiflage. Quango. Recidivist. Supine. Schism. Serendipity. Snood. Tendentious. Tautology. Ubiquitous. Venal. Water (we put that one in to encourage you). Xenophobia. Yarborough or Zoo (another easy one, so you don't feel entirely inadequate).

Well, now, THAT's put you in your place, hasn't it!? So get that toilet dictionary, and start pouring over it (not literally).

Origami

Origami – what is it?

What *is* Origami? Well, it is the ancient art of making three-dimensional models out of a single piece of paper; which makes it an ideal skill to be developed in the toilet, a place where not only will you find peace and tranquillity but also (hopefully) an abundance of paper. It is not merely a 'decorative' art. Once proficient you can use it to help you out of any number of potentially difficult and embarrassing situations. For example, if you arrive at your grandmother's house only to find that it is her birthday and you have forgotten to buy her a present, excuse yourself and politely scamper into the WC. Within minutes you will be scampering out again and handing her a tiny life-size replica of a praying mantis. She will smile and thank you and never realise how close you came to disappointing her on her special day.

You might find yourself in a restaurant that won't let you in without a tie. A quick visit to the Men's Room and the forgotten item will have miraculously appeared in the shape of a powder-blue perforated 'slim-Jim'.

You may be attending a wedding and arrive at the church only to discover that you should be wearing a hat. Ask the Vicar if you can use the vestry convenience and whilst you are in there, whip yourself up a little Samurai Sun Bonnet. You will then not only be able to cross the threshold with pride but your superb millinery style will be the envy of one and all.

But we must start at the beginning and with 'Origami' all you begin with is the paper.

The paper

You will find on the whole that people tend to use one of two types of toilet paper. For 'Origami' each has its advantages and disadvantages. The most common is the soft, pastel-shaded, two-ply, perforated roll. This is very pretty and comes in many colours but it is also floppy and difficult to fold accurately. You would be advised to stick to making flowers, dolls' clothes or, with the aid of a 'cotton bud', the spectacular 'Butterfly' (see fig. 8).

If you wish to make sturdier models you will be better off using the more 'papery' type of toilet paper. This is most often found in public toilets but is available for home use and can be purchased from most larger supermarkets and hardware stores. It folds well and will not wilt. (Come to think of it, it's far better suited to 'Origami' than its intended function.)

There are actually two types of this paper. The first is a little box full of single squares. These are perfect for small models. The second type is the supposedly perforated roll. This is ideal for long sinuous creations (the perforations rarely work anyway so you can tear off sections of any length you choose). The other advantage of this kind of paper is that its translucent texture can sometimes take on the appearance of solid marble. This can make some models look very impressive indeed (see Taj Mahal, fig. 8).

One of the most sound reasons for using your 'toilet-time' in pursuit of origamic perfection is that you can do it in any toilet – at home, at work, or out shopping – providing that the WC you find yourself in has paper (if it hasn't, turn to page 77). You don't need to take in any peripheral equipment; you won't make any noise; you can't make a mess; and mistakes need never be wasted – you can always unfold and use them for their original purpose. (Indeed, you will find the texture of coarse toilet paper will be rendered much more pleasant for having been crinkled up.) Best of all though, you will be leaving behind a little something for others to gaze at and admire. . . .

The folding

Now here are some simple basic ideas to start you off. These are the standard folds from which all origami shapes originate. Take it slowly, fold carefully and accurately, and once you have mastered the basic technique you can use it to make any number of creations of your very own.

THE SPECTACULAR BUTTERFLY

A sheet of 'soft' toilet paper

Twist centre of paper

Attach cotton bud *The Spectacular Butterfly*

MOTHER HUBBARD'S DOG

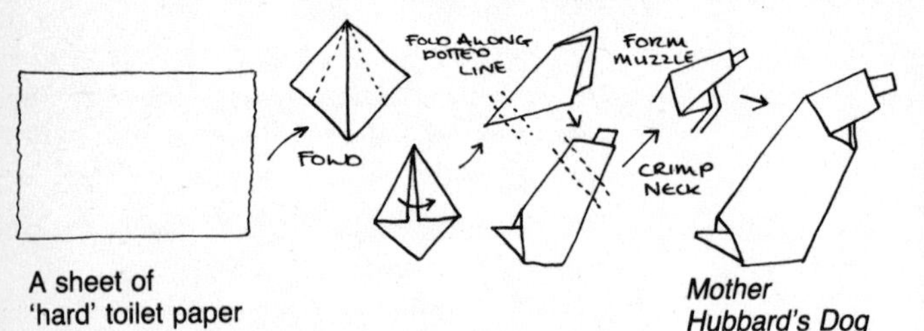

A sheet of 'hard' toilet paper

Mother Hubbard's Dog

THE TAJ MAHAL

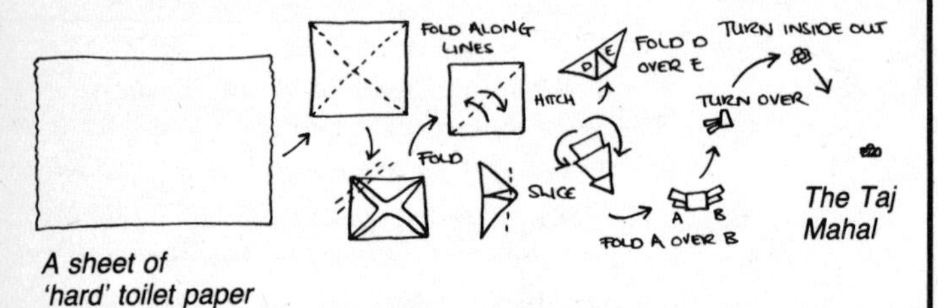

A sheet of 'hard' toilet paper

The Taj Mahal

THE SNAKE

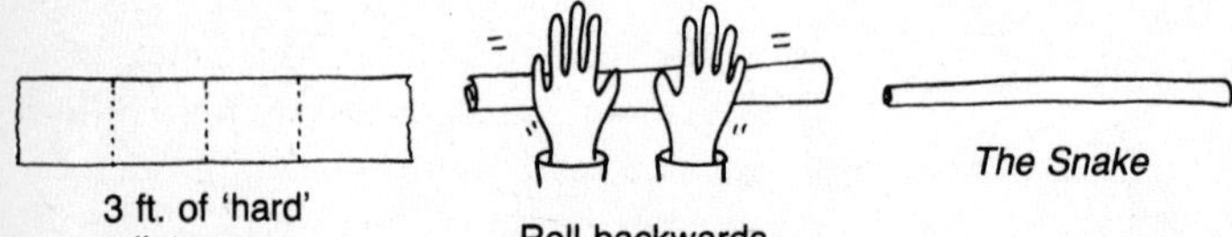

3 ft. of 'hard' toilet paper

Roll backwards and forwards

The Snake

Fig. 8.

Model-making

This is a quite different artistic medium to that of 'origami', although a combination of the two can produce some delightful results.

For 'model-making' the combined toilet/bathroom is a preferable location. Not only is it comfortable and spacious, but you will also find it a veritable 'Aladdin's Cave' of potential modelling materials; the most interesting of which can usually be found whilst rummaging through the wastepaper bin.

There are many types of models that you can attempt in the time you spend in the toilet. They range from the ever popular 'soap carvings', that can be completed in one sitting, to large-scale constructions that can be added to on every visit.

We know of a man who, in only six months, completed a life-size model of Elvis Presley constructed entirely from cotton buds and toothpaste. He positioned a small and inexpensive tape recorder in the head, which, due to some mechanical wizardry caused the apparition to give a rendition of 'Blue Suede Shoes' every time someone raised the lid of the toilet.

The resemblance, some say, was chilling.

But you really don't have to go that far. As always we must *start small.*

Making the models

There are a few items that you will always find in a toilet/bathroom, e.g. soap, toothpaste, used dental floss etc. These will be the backbone of your craft. After a while you will come to know them and their uses.

These items will look completely at home when used in the construction of 'free form' large displays, whilst retaining a potential when used on their own.

Here are a few suggestions to get you started. Once you get the idea perhaps you would like to think up some for yourself.

The models we have shown here are rather complex, but with care and patience you can slowly build up to them. As you can see there is a lot of scope and you will discover all kinds of different possibilities in each new bathroom/toilet you visit.

You will find model-making a marvellously satisfying art and you will be surprised how impressed people will be at the results. Say, for example, you are at a party and you feel you are not making any headway. For some reason, you don't seem to be creating a good impression at all. People seem to find you dull or even irksome. Don't despair.

When you eventually find yourself cowering in the bathroom/toilet, use this time and what you can see around you to construct an elaborate model of the type shown opposite. Place it somewhere where it can be seen to its best advantage and just watch people's expressions when you come rushing out of the toilet with a jubilant cry of 'Hey everyone . . . look what I've done!!'

VASE OF FLOWERS AND MOUSE

Fill the inside of a toilet roll, about halfway up, with cotton wool. Jam origami flowers on to cotton buds and place in 'vase'. Carve your soap mousey with nail file and, with the aid of a hairpin, stick used dental floss in back for tail. Grips and pins can make eyes/nose etc.

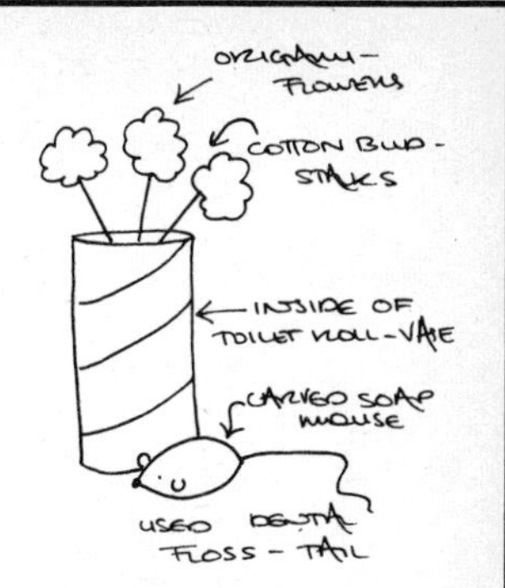

SAMMY THE SHEEP

Cover the outside of the inside of a toilet roll with toothpaste. Lay on some cotton wool. Press it down securely. Jam a 'carved soap' sheep's face (use nailfile for carving) into one end of toilet roll, and a cotton-wool ball in the other. Pierce 4 'corners' of toilet roll with nailfile and squeeze in cotton-bud legs.

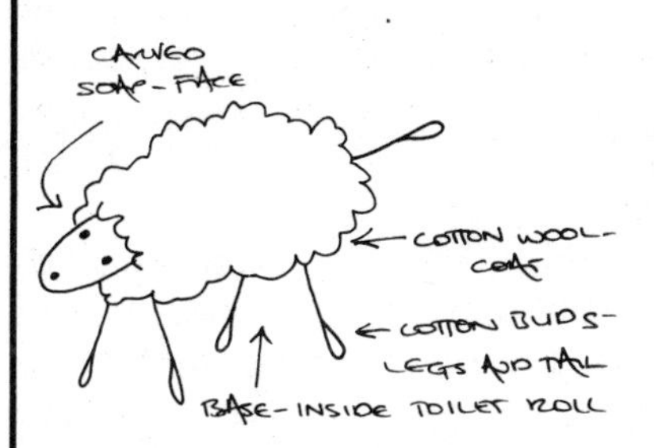

DOOM

This is more of a 'free form' toilet model. Carve the screaming face out of soap. Hollow the head out like a cracked egg. Fill the hollow with toothpaste (preferably blue) to represent the brains spilling out all over the place. Tie 3 'insides of toilet rolls' together with as much used dental floss as is available. Place around the head. Attach cotton wool to insides of toilet roll with a few blobs of toothpaste, making absolutely sure that it is completely over the top.

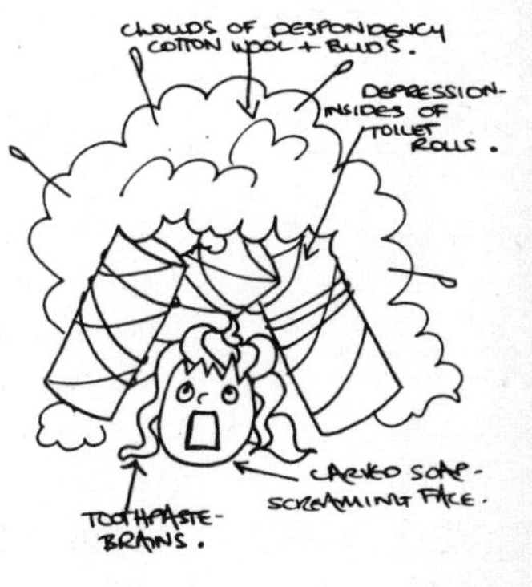

Fig. 9.

How to improve your memory

Do you find that there are certain things you can never seem to be able to remember? For example:

your passport number
your car registration number
your national insurance number
important phone numbers
which day the dustmen come
people you are introduced to at parties

How often have you found yourself being introduced to a group of smiling individuals only to look up at them five seconds later and not remember *one* of their names?

You then have the uncomfortable task of spending the rest of the evening avoiding addressing them by name, although they are managing to use yours at every opportunity. At some point some 'acquaintance' will inevitably sidle up and make the dreaded request: 'Well, aren't you going to introduce me to your friends, then?'

The nameless ones beam at you in eager anticipation.

At this point you can do one of two things: (1) Fall over or (2) clutch your stomach and mutter: 'Excuse me, I just have to go to the bathroom. . . .' Where, with any luck, you will find this book.

Once in the haven of the toilet you would do well to reflect on such events and take steps to ensure that they do not occur ever again.

This is much easier than you think. You are already halfway there in your choice of location. All you need now to improve your retention ability is a small amount of the time you spend every day in the toilet and a little bit of concentration. The results can be almost instantaneous. You can enter the toilet with no idea of your car registration number and leave never being able to forget it.

Our method is simple, straightforward and suitable for the most sieve-like memory. Follow the rules carefully and you can't go wrong.

Numbers

Remembering anything is usually a matter of word association. One's memory is often jogged by the sight of some object that at some time was instrumental in some long forgotten event.

People have difficulty memorising numbers because they have no physical identity that one can relate to, therefore they don't easily make an impression.

We will give them an identity and from now on you must remember them as such.

0	Bristol Rovers	6	Pick up Sticks
1	Singular Sensation	7	Dwarves
2	Turtle Doves	8	Maids a' Milking
3	Little Maids from School	9	Ladies Dancing
4	Tops	10	Bo Derek
5	Gold Rings		

(As you can see, the song 'Twelve Days of Christmas' comes in quite handy for this!)

So, now, instead of a cluster of numbers you have a line of delightful images which you will find much easier to remember, especially – and this is the trick – if you turn them into a story. For example, the number 847 6110 becomes: 'A milkmaid found a top and a dwarf picked up a stick and had a singular sensation with Bo Derek.'

See . . . it's much easier.

Now use the same image for every number you have to remember, whatever the permutation, and not only will you have no more trouble bringing to mind those dreaded digits but you can keep your children entertained in the process!

Letters

By far the easiest way to remember 'letters' is to associate them with a word they begin with, for example, A – apple, B – ball etc. You can then use them in the same way as we did with the numbers. Here are the words you will, from now on, associate the letters of the alphabet with:

A	anteater	**N**	nightingale
B	bat	**O**	oak tree
C	coconut	**P**	purse
D	duvet	**Q**	queen
E	ectoplasm	**R**	rocket
F	fairyland	**S**	sauce
G	gargoyle	**T**	toucan
H	hatter	**U**	university
I	India	**V**	vegan
J	jockstrap	**W**	windscreen
K	kiss	**X**	xylophone
L	loganberry	**Y**	yacht
M	milliner	**Z**	zebra

So if you wanted to remember your car registration number which happened to be GQA 036J, the story would be: 'A gargoyle, the queen and an anteater went to Bristol Rovers where they met three little maids from school picking up sticks with a jockstrap.'

Try the same process with any other numbers, letters or combination of both you wish to remember.

Days

Those with a thought process similar to that of René Magritte may have an advantage here. This is an infallible method of remembering which day of the week, a friend, the dustman or the window-cleaner is going to call.

Here are your word associations for days of the week:

Monday –	moustache	**Friday** –	fish
Tuesday –	tongue	**Saturday** –	sack
Wednesday –	wart-hog	**Sunday** –	submarine
Thursday –	thermos flask		

From now on *always* associate each day with its own special word. So if the dustman is coming on Wednesday keep a mental picture in your head of *a wart-hog in a dustbin*. If your friend is coming for coffee on Monday, *think about her from now on wearing a moustache*; and if the window-cleaner is coming on Saturday think of a *window with a sack in it*.

The possibilities are, as ever, endless. But now you are familiar with the technique you can apply it to anything. Months, years, special occasions and appointments. Make up your own words and charts and memorise them carefully.

Names

Now we couldn't possibly list every name there is, or this book would go on for volumes. But we can get you thinking in the right direction.

This is a slightly different process to the ones above.

Let's get back to that crowd of people at the party. First of all, when you are introduced to one or a dozen people – *concentrate*. All too often you are too busy thinking about what you are wearing, what sort of wine you want to drink or where the hostess got her loose covers from, to take any notice of what is being said, and by the time you realise, it's too late.

By far the best way of remembering Christian names is to associate them with a famous person. For example, Janis, Jack, Bob and Julie will become Janis Joplin, Jack Niklaus, Bob Hope and Julie Andrews.

Try to make yourself think of a song or an aspect of the famous person's character that is associated with them as you acknowledge the greeting of the people you are being introduced to. Janis: 'loud raucous voice'; Jack: 'Golf'; Bob: 'Thanks for the memory'; Julie: 'The Nuns' Chorus'. So from then onwards you will look at Bob and think . . . 'Thanks for the memory' – Bob Hope. Ah yes – 'Bob'.

However do be careful you don't go off in the wrong direction, for example, you may look at Donny – think 'puppy Love' – and spend the rest of the evening calling him 'Lassie'.

Tap-dancing

If you were to ask every single person in the whole wide world what it is that they would *most* like to learn if they had the money, time and space, we guarantee that they would all say the same thing: TAP-DANCING.

As ever, for all those people help is at hand. In the next few pages we will show you how you can master this coveted skill in a small space, in no time at all and without spending a penny.

The sound

We will be writing a lot in this book about covering noise, disguising noise and avoiding noise (see page 72), but as far as tap-dancing goes, it is imperative that you *make* lots of noise. Not only that, but you must be able to hear *every* sound that you make (with your feet that is). (Although any outside noise can always be incorporated into the routine – remember Fred Astaire and the *Boat Engine* routine?)

Obviously if your toilet floor is polished wood, tiles or lino you will have no problem, but if the area around your, or anybody else's, pedestal is covered in a thick, shag pile carpet, you may have difficulty telling your shuffles from your flaps. This could prove disastrous if you are in the middle of a shim-sham.

To alleviate this problem you can do this: construct your own portable 'toilet-tap-mat'. It is easy to carry, it will fit any standard pedestal and you will have no problem collapsing it for easy storage.

You can use it at home or take it with you wherever you go. And all you need to construct it is two large cardboard egg boxes.

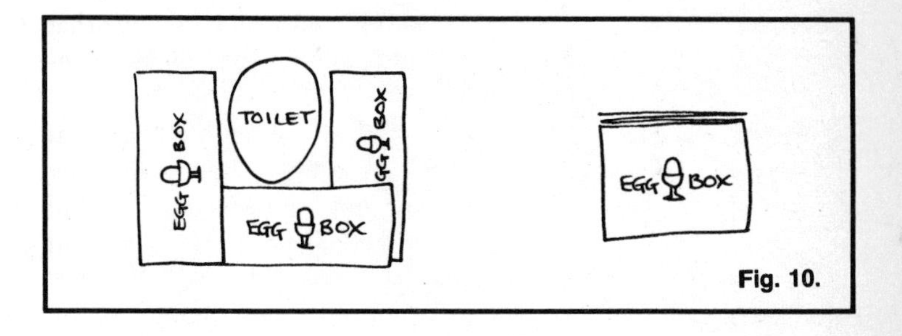

Fig. 10.

Tap shoes

For practising your toe-taps ordinary shoes are quite effective; more effective than bare feet. But with the trend today leaning towards rubber-soled trainers, deck shoes and espadrilles, all of which don't make much of an impression, let alone any noise, you may find that you have to give them a bit of a hand! This comes in the shape of four empty tooth-paste tubes which you can either save yourself or cadge from friends. Once you've explained why you need them you'll find that they will be most under-standing. Flatten them out and when you have collected your four empty tubes, attach them to your shoes with used dental floss like so:

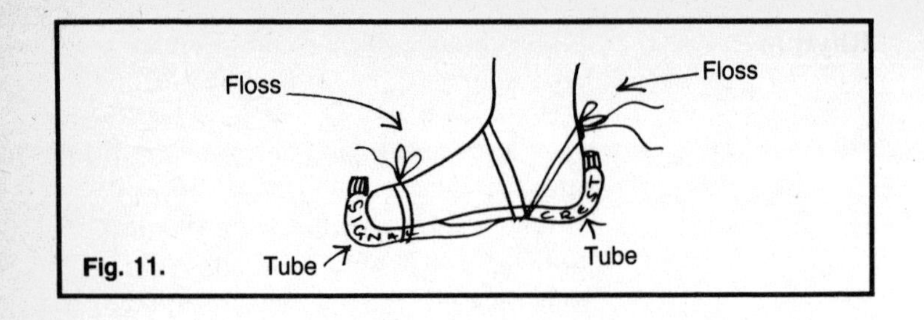

Fig. 11.

Make sure that a) you tie the floss tightly and b) the toothpaste tubes are completely empty, or else a few over-enthusiastic stamps will see toothpaste flying out all over the place! Once attached correctly, you will find the sound is quite clear and acceptable.

By far the best place to try out your newly acquired tap-shoes is the local public lavatories. The floor is usually covered in highly polished tiles and the accoustics are second to none. With any luck you may be able to find the odd busker occupying a neighbouring cubicle, whom you can tap along to. And if it's a Saturday night you may even find yourself alongside a whole band! You'll be astounded at the difference that will make!

The groundwork

The first steps towards emulating such as the Nicolas Brothers will be to remove your trousers and pants completely. This way your legs and feet are free to move around the pedestal and attempt movements such as 'side-splits' and 'trenches'.

It must be said that, for tap-dancing, the No. 2 toilet position is infinitely preferable to the No. 1 which can be rather messy.

Rhythm

Now you are sitting comfortably, arms relaxed, toes at the ready, you must find a rhythm. Listen. Can you hear a dripping tap? A whirling extractor fan? A ticking clock?

Now click your fingers to a sound . . . both hands. Now the feet . . . tap along . . . first the right foot . . . tap it from side to side . . . now the left foot. Now both together . . . tap, tap, tap, eight on the left . . . eight on the right . . . four on the left . . . four on the right . . . keep those fingers clicking . . . two on the left, two on the right. Move your shoulders backwards and forwards. Use your whole body, remembering that your hands and face are just as important as your feet. Now you are in the mood, try the exercises, diagrams and routines illustrated below . . . AND KEEP SMILING!

kick
Clap kicks
Tap Tap
Shim-Sham
Tap Tap
Tap
Shuffle
Shuffles
Tap
Flaps
TAP-DANCING: FIVE BASIC MOVES
(Put them together and create a *really* impressive routine)
Tap Tap
Tap Tap Tap
Trenches

Fig. 12.

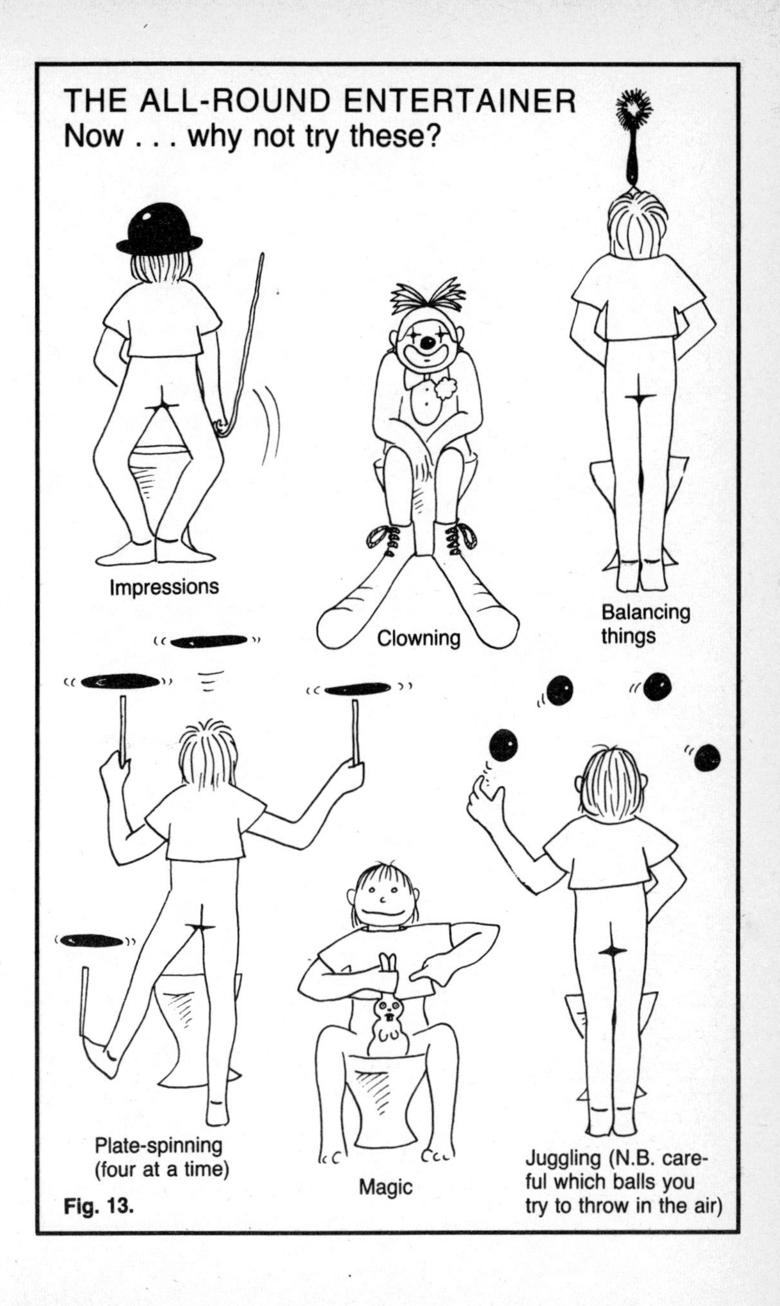
THE ALL-ROUND ENTERTAINER
Now . . . why not try these?
Impressions
Clowning
Balancing things
Plate-spinning (four at a time)
Magic
Juggling (N.B. careful which balls you try to throw in the air)
Fig. 13.

Useless skills

This is of course a playful contradiction in terms. We do not consider the acquisition of any skill to be useless, as it is bound to be both therapeutic and entertaining. It is surely not useless to be able to give pleasure and provoke laughter, and most of us remember with delight the jolly uncle who used to enthral us when we were little children by wiggling his ears or pretending to pull off our noses. Now we are grown-ups ourselves, maybe our fascination has turned to envy that our own kids prefer their jolly uncle to their boring parents.

'But he's so funny,' they taunt us. 'Why can't *you* raise one eyebrow and turn *your* lips inside out, like *Uncle* can?' 'Yes, well *Uncle* doesn't have to go out to work to earn money to buy school clothes for you, does he? I only wish *I* had the *time* to practise wiggling *my* ears!'

Well, you *have* got the time – and you know when it is, don't you? And you know where.

Now own up, the reason you don't do what Uncle does is because you *can't*. And you're scared to try in case you look *silly*. Well, there's no more appropriate place to look silly than in the toilet, where we all look pretty daft to start with. So come on, get wiggling and put that uppity uncle in his place. . . .

Ultimately, we can't *really* tell you how to accomplish many of these useless (but satisfying) skills. You all know the effects you're after, so it's just a matter of sitting there and willing yourself into achieving them. If at all possible make sure you can see the results reflected in a mirror. You may well *feel* that you're wiggling your ears when in fact you're not, and your children will respect you even less if you rush out of the toilet yelling, 'Hey kids, look what I can do' and then stand there totally motionless, pointing at your own head with a stupid grin on your face.

Here is a selection from Uncle's repertoire that you may care to try, with their techniques explained as best we can.

Wiggling your ears If you're doing it right, it hurts. Unless you are experiencing the symptoms of severe migraine they're probably not visibly moving. Think: 'Wiggle wiggle flap flap'.

Turning your lips inside out

Pull the lower lip down over your chin and leave it there. Now firmly grip the upper lip and hook it over your nose. Wrinkle your nose in order to keep it (the lip) in position. Do not sneeze, or you'll split your face in two. The children might like that, but you won't.

Touching your nose with your tongue

Open your mouth and stick out your tongue as far as possible. Now curl it upwards and try to touch the tip of the nose with the tip of the tongue. If you need an incentive, try sticking a half-sucked fruit gum on the end of your nose.

Going cross-eyed

Pick up the loo brush and hold it at arm's length. Fix your eyes on the circular spikey bit at the tip. Bring the brush closer and closer to your face, until your nose is poking through the circular spiky bit (in the mirror, this should look as if you're eating a hedgehog). If you've kept your eyes on the brush they should now be crossed. Eventually you should be able to do it without any artificial aid – children will *not* be impressed if you always have to use the loo brush. If you experience difficulty, try to condition yourself to go cross-eyed merely by thinking about the brush.

WARNING – you may begin to react the same way to hedgehogs; which could be very dangerous when driving.

Raising one eyebrow

This is a great test of mental discipline. It is a well known fact that different areas of the brain control different emotions. The cells governing stress and worry are located on the right side of the cranium, whilst the cells registering surprise are on the left (which is why most people who *can* raise one eyebrow find it easier to raise the left).

You must literally split your personality. With the right side of your brain think about your tax returns, and your right eyebrow will knit. With the left side imagine Mary Whitehouse doing a strip-tease and your left eyebrow will shoot upwards. Or possibly both eyes will close. In which case, try the physical approach. Paint one eyebrow with superglue and try raising them both.

Combining the effects

You may care to see off that bleedin' uncle once and for all. Spend as much time as you can secretly practising in the toilet, to the point where the children have forgotten you exist. Wait for a day when Uncle is entertaining the whole family by pretending to unscrew his head. Imagine their surprise when you leap out of the loo displaying *all your abilities at the same time!* Eyes crossed, with one brow raised, ears wiggling, tongue protruding, lips turned inside out with a fruit gum on the end of your nose. Uncle will never compete for your children's affections again – especially if he has a weak heart.

Extending your range

There are of course all manner of useless skills you could attempt in the toilet. At least half the fun (if not all of it) will be thinking up your own. Here are just a few more to start the ball rolling:

1 Ball rolling

Further suggestions

What we have shown you in the previous chapters should occupy your toilet-time for at least three or four years. After that, you're on your own. (Personally we think three years' worth is pretty good considering this is a very cheap little book.) In fact you should have no difficulty thinking up lots and lots more exciting and deeply satisfying new activities. If you *do* have difficulty, think along these lines:

1. Things you've *always* wanted to be able to do (no matter how trivial or silly) . . . like playing the musical saw, or picking up pennies with your toes.
2. Things you can *never* remember or wish you knew . . . such as basic geography – where exactly *is* Saudi Arabia, or El Salvador? – and history – precisely how fat *is* Prince William?
3. Little jobs you always wish you had time for – sewing, needlework, home-welding, do it yourself acupuncture and so on. . . .

Remember, if they can be done in 11½ minutes, you can do them TODAY.
Make sure you EQUIP your loo to its

maximum potential; and become TOILET-AWARE.

As an inspiration we end this section by offering you our artists' impression of

THE IDEAL TOILET

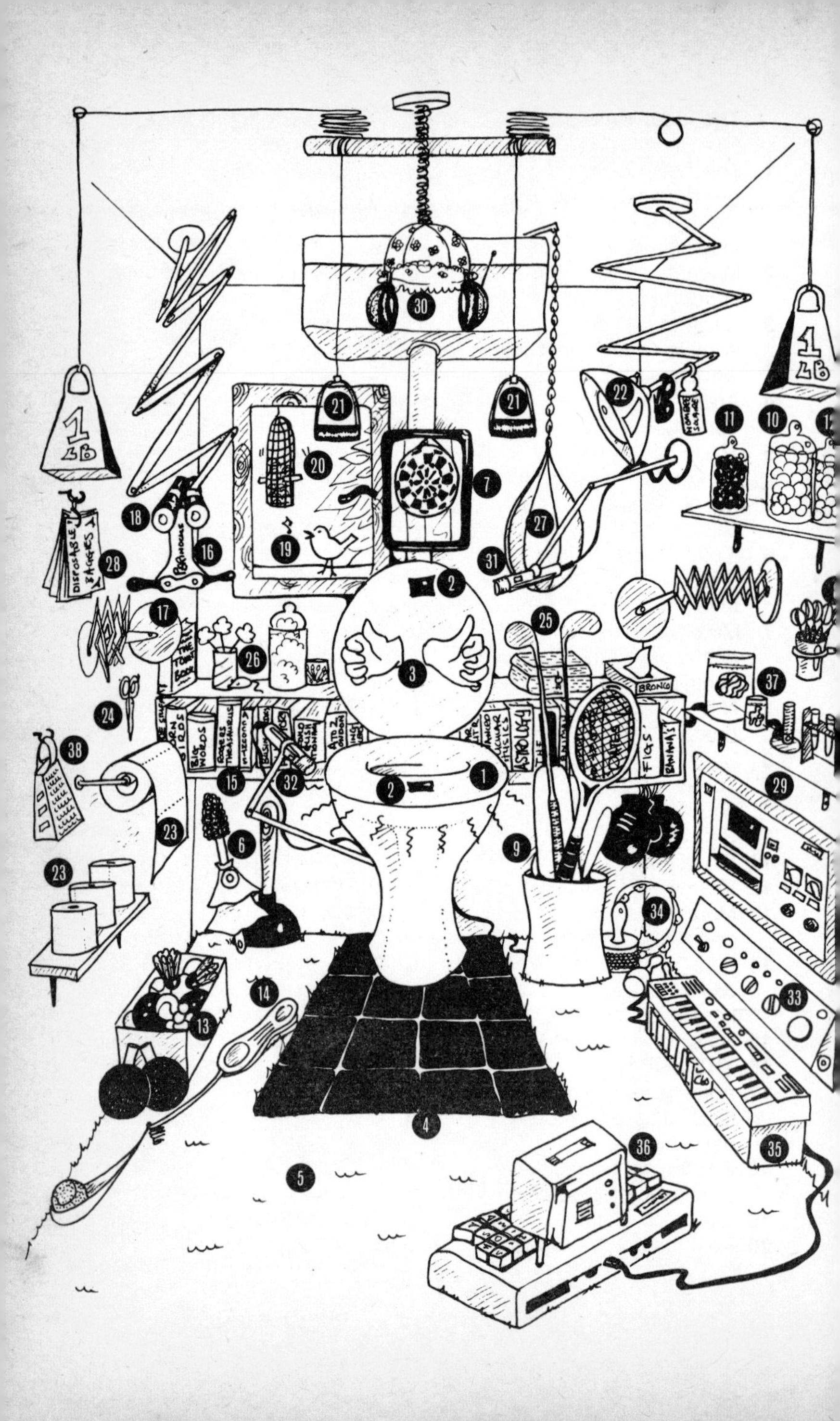
1 LB
1 LB
DISPOSABLE BAGGIES
THE TOILET BOOK
BIG WORDS
ROGERS THESAURUS
A TO Z LONDON
ASTROLOGY
FIGS
BANANA'S
BRONCO
1
2
3
4
5
6
7
9
10
11
13
14
15
16
17
18
19
20
21
22
23
24
25
26
27
28
29
30
31
32
33
34
35
36
37
38

The Ideal Toilet

1 Toilet seat made of galvanised 'comfi-sit' rubber. Internal electric coil provides gentle heating
2 Magnets to keep the seat lifted, for gentlemen
3 Electronic fingers provide soothing back massage while-u-visit
4 Area of tiles for tap-dancing
5 Thick pile carpet for golf or comfy landing if you fall off the loo doing exercises
6 'Lotty Loo Brush' and 'Plungo' – for ventriloquism
7 Mirror above toilet – for gentlemen to practise ventriloquial exercises. N.B. Reflection of dartboard
8 Darts
9 Sports equipment – bats and racquets
10 Ping Pong Balls
11 Squash Balls
12 Vitamin Pills
13 More balls . . . for bowls or skittles
14 Foot pedal to release cricket ball for wicket-keeper practice
15 Reference books
16 **THE TOILET BOOK**
17 Adjustable mirrors – for facial exercise, grooming, narcissism etc.
18 Periscopic binoculars for on-the-loo bird-watching
19 Bird
20 Peanuts to attract bird
21 Weighted handles for arm exercises
22 Sun-ray lamp
23 Paper – for toilet-use and origami
24 Scissors – for model-making, needlework etc.
25 Sewing box
26 Examples of model work
27 Punchball
28 Disposable bags in case you overdo exercise work
29 Multi-track cassette recorder for playback for tap-dancing, or recording vocals over pre-recorded backing tracks. Remember, the acoustics are excellent in here
30 Earphones for listening to playback (light flex is adjustable and retractable)
31 Microphone for recording vocals (and interesting thoughts)
32 Microphone connected to . . .
33 Synthesizer. This will translate toilet sounds into amazing musical effects
34 Percussion for overdubs
35 Keyboard – can be played with toes of left foot (right foot is used for operating cricket balls)
36 Computer (can be operated with both feet when not playing keyboard or cricket)
37 Pickled brain and test-tubes – for scientific experiments
38 Cheese-grater

Part Two

Other people's toilets

An instant trouble-shooting guide to problems and emergencies

IMPORTANT If you are in trouble at this very moment and have had to turn to this page immediately – now turn to the *next* page immediately, and identify your particular problem. Then, once you've solved it, go back to page 3 and enjoy *Part One*.

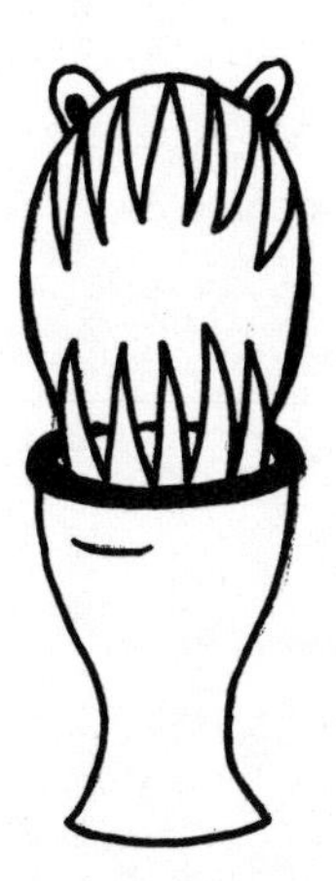

Just when you thought it was safe to go . . .

List of contents – (continued)

Part Two Other people's toilets

The terror of the toilet

The responsible toilet owner will equip his or her loo meticulously so that it is totally relaxing, efficient and potentially instructive. The 'mechanics' of the system should be maintained and serviced as thoroughly and regularly as a motor car. If this is done properly then your toilet will be a joy and inspiration to yourself and a delight to others. If you have bought this book, appreciated its instruction, and absorbed its spirit then no doubt your own toilet will be beyond criticism. Alas, not everyone will be so enlightened.

Using **other people's toilets** can be a nightmare. They are rarely as well appointed as your own; they probably have limited or defective facilities; and they are intimidatingly unfamiliar. Using even the best of them is likely to be unrelaxing; using the worst of them can be hell.

The most unnerving aspect of going to the toilet at somebody else's house is that it is an almost public experience – there are other people present to judge your performance, watching you as you come out, waiting to go in next, and possibly even listening to what you're doing whilst you're in there. Things you would do shamelessly at home do not come so easily when you are 'out'. We assume that most of you, like us, are basically slightly 'coy'. We are not actually embarrassed at asking 'Where's the loo?' or indeed admitting that we need to use it, though the requests can be confusingly oblique (see page 95 – 'Euphemisms'). However, most of us do wish the operation to be quick, clean, quiet and discreet.

The more intimate and refined the social event the more concerned is the toilet-goer that his or her activity should be accomplished with speed and dignity. There are, alas, many many things that can **go wrong** and lots of potential **embarrassments** and indeed **dangers**.

Many of these may be obliterated by the hurly-burly of a full-scale party – if everyone else is smashed out of their heads you'll be able to get away with most things. However, at a dinner party or afternoon tea you are much more vulnerable, and going to the toilet can represent as daunting a prospect as crossing Niagara Falls sitting in a barrel (not an entirely inappropriate image, come to think of it).

A cursory glance at the next pages will indicate just how many pitfalls there are and may induce such a state of nervous paranoia that you'll become permanently constipated. This could avoid an awful lot of problems, but may cause others. Our intention is to help the toilet-goer achieve relief and satisfaction, with the minimum of fuss or embarrassment so that his or her time spent in the smallest room can be productive and self-improving.

The following pages are intended as a practical guide to whatever predicament you may find yourself in future or may be in **right now**. Each section is clearly captioned with a heading allowing you to locate your particular problem. Key words are rendered in **bold type** so you can further identify your **specific dilemma** and quickly attempt a **solution**. If you have sufficient time or foresight we suggest you read the whole thing **before** your next toilet-visit and you may thereby do yourself a big favour. You will, we hope, find our treatment all-embracing and sympathetic. However, if you are actually in a toilet at this **very moment** and in trouble **right now** skip the introductions and anecdotes and home in on the **bold type** before it's **too late**.

Whatever your plight, salvation is nigh. . . .

No lock

The terror of finding **no lock** on a toilet door can stem from very early childhood. The fragmented images of sinister uncles 'accidently' walking in on you lurk in the shadows of your memory only to be summoned once more to your consciousness by the sight of an unlockable toilet door.

Sitting on a toilet you are at your most vulnerable. Not only that but you are totally trapped. Once your bladder or bowels are moving, *you* are most definitely not. You have to sit tight, until the ingenious bodily function has run its course.

It's a time when you should be able to relax, ponder over the day's events, review your situation and practise your skills (see pages 3 to 55), not sit there like a demented, gibbering wreck, hardly daring to move, let alone evacuate, your eyes unblinkingly staring at the door handle, waiting for the slightest movement or the sound of the inevitable, approaching footsteps. The cry sticks in the back of your throat, perspiration forms a relief map on your forehead, the handle turns, you reach out towards it but the door is too far away . . . it slowly creaks open . . . and there, in the doorway stands Michael Jackson, E.T., and the entire cast from *Dallas* and all you can do is . . . **sit there with your pants round your ankles!!!!**

We have all had this nightmare, waking or sleeping. So why is it that some people still don't bother to ensure that there is a lock on their toilet door? It is quite unbelievable.

Admittedly it can be an error, a misplaced key or recently broken bolt. On some occasions you will find that the toilet owner is concerned that their immature offspring may obtain possession of the key and shut themselves in or everyone else out. This theory is substantiated by an incident recounted to us by a dear friend.

The incident concerned a three-year-old child who had locked himself in a third floor WC. After much cajoling and pleading from his family, and little or no luck, the child's father eventually decided to attempt to climb up the drainpipe at the back of the house and somehow clamber through the small square toilet window.

Six minutes after the distraught father had begun his hair-raising ascent, the small child managed to turn the key, his mother opened the door and the delighted family bore the young lad into the sitting-room, whereupon they celebrated his return to the fold with cups of tea and battenburg cake, completely forgetting about the clambering master of the house who by this time was three-quarters of the way up the rusting drainpipe.

Needless to say, a visiting aunt, just back from a shopping expedition and unaware of the drama that had preceded her arrival, slipped into the WC to 'powder her nose'. (She wasn't really going to powder her nose. See page 95 – 'Euphemisms'.) The rather prim and rotund lady had just about got herself settled into place, pulled out a copy of *The Sporting Life*, when a hand appeared on the window sill, then another. Then an exhausted slobbering face rose up between them.

This sudden and unexpected sight caused the startled woman to let forth a reverberating 'botty burp' (see page 95 again) and the unfortunate man to slide back down the drainpipe like something out of a Laurel and Hardy movie.

If nothing else, stories like this do teach one to keep one's eyes on small children and square toilet windows.

Sometimes, though, the lack of a lock or bolt on a toilet door can be completely intentional. We have heard that some 'free-thinking' families have no compunction whatsoever about not only leaving locks off doors but leaving their toilet doors wide open! They will take in their jasmine tea, read *The Hobbit*, wave to passers-by and even hold house meetings in the occupied smallest room.

News has also reached us of new modern open-plan houses that are being built in Sweden, with toilets that have no door on them at all – not even a beaded curtain! (In some cases the pedestal is 'free-standing' in the middle of the living-room or kitchen.)

Well, each to his own . . . and if you happen to have one of these 'devil may care' attitudes towards toilet-going then read no further. However, if like us, you cherish those private moments . . . read on.

As always the most hazardous and difficult TOILET TRIPS occur at **parties** or **gatherings**. It is here that the ultimate nightmare can occur. You have established that the only WC in the house is unlockable and you are not familiar enough with any other 'party guest' to request that they **stand guard**. Moreover, the unlockable WC is situated in a crowded hallway. Nevertheless you are desperate so you dive inside. Another guest, unaware that the toilet is in use, opens the door and has his or her attention immediately distracted. They then stand there holding the DOOR OPEN, gabbling on to someone about the calories found in a portion of Cod in Shrimp Sauce, while you sit, knicks round ankles, in full view of a hall full of laughing, chatting party-goers.

Even if they do eventually hear your feeble cries of 'Excuse me . . . would you mind closing the door please?' it is by this time too late. Your evening is ruined. How can you confidently face the tasty bloke you've been rolling your eyes at all evening now he's seen you doing wee wees (no need to see page 95)?

You may think it's too late, but the time to become **toilet-aware** is now!

What you can do to avoid situations like the one above really depends on the design of the toilet you find yourself in (see fig 1 – 'Typical Toilets').

The old **leg up** (See figs (a) & (b) overleaf) is a widely used and very handy method of keeping an unlocked door closed; providing the door is close enough and **opens inwards.**

If, however, the door opens **outwards** you are in trouble. You are then not only **discovered** squatting on a WC but you will also have one leg up in the air. For ladies in figs (a) and (c) 'leg up' position and men in fig (a) 'leg up' position, the posture can be fairly easily explained as pronounced **cramp** in one leg. For men in

FOUR BASIC LEG-UP POSITIONS

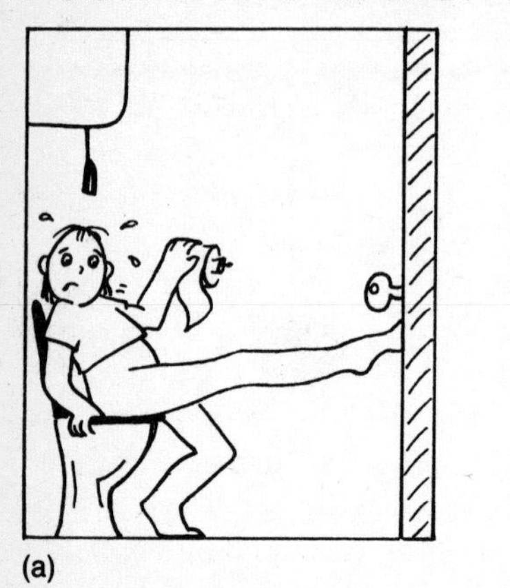
(a)

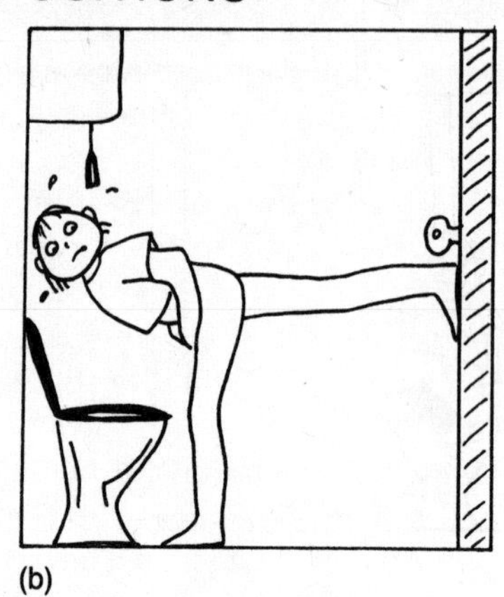
(b)

N.B. Make *absolutely certain* that the door (or doors) open *inwards*

the fig (b) 'leg up' position the explanations are slightly less easy, unless you have already mentioned to the assembled throng that you are a **ballet dancer**.

But the problem *really* begins when you find that your extremities are in no way extreme enough to cope with the amount of space between you and the dreaded unlocked door. Now is the time to **look around**.

Can you see a **toilet-brush**, a **broom**, a **mop**? A small **towel**? A small but fairly heavy bathroom **cabinet**? Are you wearing a **jacket**, a **cardigan**, a pair of **tights** or **belt**?

Depending on which way the door opens you can use the above to do the following:

1 *Doors opening outwards from your Point of View.*

a Tie tights, belt, cardigan or jacket securely round door handle, making sure that you can hold the other end quite comfortably. Pull tightly until you are ready to leave the room.

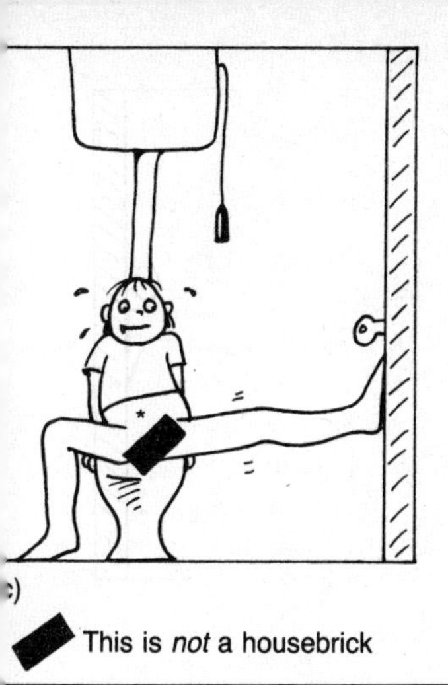

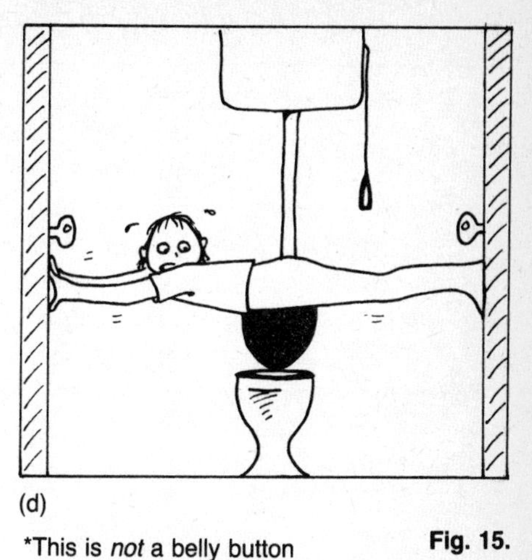

(c) (d)

This is *not* a housebrick *This is *not* a belly button **Fig. 15.**

2 *Doors opening inwards from your Point of View.*

a Use toilet brush, mop, broom to hold against door and push hard until the toilet operation is completed.

b Use small towel (or articles in 1 (a)) to cram under door and wedge it shut.

c Place small heavy cabinet in front of door and hope that no one pushes it too hard.

If you are lucky you will find one or other of these articles in the WC you have found yourself in, but if your host omitted to fit a lock on the door it's quite likely that this particular 'smallest room' could be pretty **shoddily equipped**.

It may be too late now but for future visits to other people's houses, parties or pubs make sure you leave the house **prepared**. Take:

1 a strong crooked **walking-stick**
2 a **wedge**
3 a length of **rope**

You may have to conceal these items on your person if you do not think you can fabricate a convincing enough explanation for their presence.

The wedge is no problem either way and can be slipped into a pocket quite discreetly.

The rope can be tied round one's waist under a voluminous blouson and explained as the few pounds you put on whilst you were on holiday. Alternatively, you can loop it round your shoulder and enter the room with the opening line 'Phew! . . . nearly didn't get here; been **mountain climbin'** all day!' At which you may be lucky and people will just smile and nod and hand you a glass of dry sherry and a canapé; or alternatively you may be less lucky and Sir Edmund Hillary may appear from the bustling crowd and propel you into a corner to discuss the pros and cons of crampons. Is it worth the risk?

Personally, we would favour the extra pounds and the blouson. There's nothing people like better than seeing someone else put on weight. You'll be the hit of the evening, and have no worries about the WC either.

Which brings us to the walking-stick. Explaining a walking-stick isn't too difficult. A well-acted **limp** should do the trick but it's exhausting to keep it up all evening – and easy to forget. It's also less convincing if you've used the 'mountain climbing' ruse already. The alternative is to slip the walking-stick down one **trouser leg**. Then, not only will you be able to rest easy in the knowledge that your toilet-going will be undisturbed but you may also find yourself quite a hit with the ladies (if you're a man that is).

Once inside the unlockable toilet, with rope, stick and wedge you are covered at every turn. For doors that open inwards you have your wedge and your walking-stick. For doors that open outwards, you have your rope tied round the handle.

A couple of handy hints if, for some reason, you should be **caught** with rope or stick in hand (say, for example, you have misjudged the door-opening direction). Immediately the door opens, shove the free end of the rope **in your mouth** and explain that you were trying to pull a **tooth**.

The presence of the stick can be explained as the legacy of a **sporting accident**, or the solution to an inability to touch your private parts due to a mysterious **rash** you contracted in Havana.

Of course the one danger of becoming a master or mistress of the art of keeping the door shut is that in your smugness you may forget that others may not be so skilful. Just remember this when you swan into the unlockable loo for the second time. There may be someone in there already: and if there's one thing almost as embarrassing as having someone burst in on you – it's when *you* burst in on someone else. Embarrassment is all the more mortifying if it remains silent, therefore someone must *say something*. It is simply not reasonable to expect the person crouching there in an exposed and vulnerable posture to instantly come up with some slick or witty remark to diffuse the mutual discomfort – therefore **toilet etiquette** dictates that it is the intruder who must speak first . . . and indeed last. Do not attempt to hold a conversation. Just deliver a short, flippant and yet sympathetic line, close the door and go away – right away if possible. It is only good manners to leave the party and if possible the country, thus avoiding any risk of seeing the person you walked in on ever again.

The pain of your exile will be much relieved by the knowledge that you left the exposed toilet-goer entirely at ease by your parting remark, which could have been any one of the following:

What to say

'It's OK – we all do it.'

Or: 'Don't worry – you can come and watch me any time.'

'Goodbye.'

Or, if you want to be *really* considerate, why not try:

'Excuse me, have you seen my guide dog?' (To complete the effect you should then walk straight into a wall and fall down stairs; audibly.)

What not to say

There may be other acceptable remarks but the following are definitely *not* amongst them:

'Gor blimey, look at the state of that!'

'Good grief, they've got spots on!' (Whatever this refers to it's humiliating.)

Or: 'Don't worry, you've got nothing to hide!'

Nor on any account should you point and fall about laughing or go: 'Poooooooooh!. . . .'

The seat

By and large toilet seats are not a great cause of distress, and indeed they may be a great source of comfort. Nevertheless, it is worth **inspecting them** before you sit down. Not long ago the vast majority of seats were made of hard durable plastic of which the only possible defect was that it might **warp** slightly, especially if the toilet was close to the hot water pipes. Sitting on a misshapen seat is rather a pleasant and unusually sensual experience, and it's not dangerous even if it wobbles; unless you wobble off on to the hot pipes.

Recent trends, however, have introduced two fashionable materials – stripped pine and pneumatic PVC – both of which you're likely to find behind a toilet door that has no lock on it. Both have flaws.

Wood can of course produce **splinters**, and it also develops **cracks**. Usually these are not big enough to trap anything really vital, but they can give you a nasty nip on the backside. A pair of **tweezers**, a small piece of **sandpaper**, and a tube of **Polyfilla** should smooth out any problems. **Carry them always**.

The Pneumatic PVC – usually in lurid colours – is not actually dangerous but it is very *clammy* and can adhere to bare flesh in a quite unpleasant manner. In fact it can stick so securely that, if you're there for a long time, when you get up you might take the seat with you. It is therefore worth carefully **disengaging** your behind before rising. PVC seats also make **rude noises** if you shift position – like wriggling around on a leather armchair. This can be potentially embarrassing or a saving grace if you can **blame** the PVC seat for making noises you were actually responsible for yourself. (For a fuller discussion of this topic turn to page 74.)

The principal peril of a toilet seat, of whatever material, is to men who are standing up in front of it and have, like gentlemen, lifted the seat. Some seats **won't stay up**. You keep lifting it and it keeps crashing down as you get more and more desperate to start. Worse still are the ones that stay up for a few seconds – so that you have already started – and *then* crash down. Not only does this divert your spray all over the place, including yourself, but it can also slice through a sensitive area like a guillotine. The one major consolation of pneumatic PVC is that it is not so heavy and can do less damage.

There are two answers to this problem. The coward's way out (or the dare-devil's, depending on how you look at it) is not to lift the seat at all, and to rely on your **accuracy of aim** (we'd suggest you practise diligently at home). The second approach is to develop a **strict routine**, which goes like this. Do *not* immediately lift the seat. Unzip yourself with both hands. Take yourself in one hand (most people favour the left) whilst lifting the seat with the other hand – the right. Adopt a slightly hunched position and relieve yourself whilst continuing to hold the seat up with your right hand. When you have finished, **take one step back** and then and only then remove your right hand. The seat will now snap shut like a crocodile's jaws. Now readjust yourself, using both hands.

Some toilets may have loose seats and these can also pinch flesh very painfully; or they may come off altogether whilst you're using them. No one feels terribly relaxed about rejoining a dinner party brandishing a toilet seat, so it really is worth always carrying a small adjustable **monkey wrench**.

Of course there may be **no seat at all**. Considering the potential perils we have just explained this could be considered a blessing. The prospect of sitting on ice-cold porcelain may not be very inviting but surely it cannot be dangerous? Beware of complacency. Remember the circumference of the bowl will be considerably increased by its lack of seat: it is all too easy to **fall in**. Children and anorexic ladies may be in very real danger of drowning, and even plump people can easily get **stuck**. Bare flesh in contact with bare porcelain is likely to form a vacuum of air rather like a rubber plunger in a blocked sink so that even if the toilet-goer can wrench him or herself free it is likely to cause an involuntary flushing of the toilet, and if there's no lock on the door the next person might be in there before you can cover your embarrassment. If you do get **stuck** down a seatless loo, swallow your pride and **call for help**. You will have the consolation of knowing that if the seat's been off for some time you won't be the first.

The whole ghastly experience can of course be avoided by **never actually sitting down** at all. By all means adopt a sitting position, but lean slightly forward so that your weight is carried by your legs, not your behind. Make sure your feet never leave the ground (or you'll topple back and possibly in). If there is a nearby **towel rail**, hang on to it for better balance, but don't pull yourself up it when you've finished or you may wrench it out of the wall. (Re-entry to a dinner party carrying a towel rail is nearly as humiliating as carrying a toilet seat.)

Whilst we're at it, if there are any toilet-seat manufacturers reading this, we feel the ideal product would be made of washable galvanised rubber, with a low output electric heating element running through it, and a small magnet on the front edge that would connect to a metal plate on the lid, thus keeping the seat safely 'lifted' when desired.

Covering the noise

Going to the toilet is rarely an entirely silent operation. 'Number ones' are no great problem, as the sound of a gentle trickle can in no way be considered offensive, embarrassing or comical, and could even be construed as rather soothing. Men can even suppress the sound altogether if they want by directing the jet onto the porcelain rather than into the water; though their satisfaction at such an achievement may be undermined if they emerge smugly only to be asked: 'Did you actually *do* anything in there?' a question which definitely implies that they are under suspicion of abusing their host's facilities and probably themselves. By and large, then, one is best advised to **'tinkle' audibly and honestly** and 'number ones' should cause no trouble.

The sound of '**number twos**' though is quite a different matter. In the process the toilet-goer may emit a variety of **little noises** (or indeed quite big ones). They are variable, unpredictable and often uncontrollable: embarrassing to make and offensive (or hilarious) to hear. (If you don't know what we're talking about turn to page 95 for a full list of 'euphemisms'. Actually, we're sure you know perfectly well what we mean, so let's carry on. . . .)

It is important to state here and now that *everyone* does make little noises: and we do mean *everyone*. Even Princess Diana, Mary Whitehouse and the Pope. (You'll notice that of this purely random trio, two are female. This is not because women are twice as 'noisy' as men but merely to stress the fact that they *do* do it too. This is not always freely acknowledged. We did once know a woman who denied *ever* doing it at all, but we don't believe her and in fact we are perfectly sure we heard her – although it *was* only once and it was a very little noise indeed.)

Nevertheless she must have 'let one go' occasionally, and all women do, though many *men* prefer not to believe it, as if it somehow undermines the feminity of their wives, girlfriends or screen idols. Nevertheless, the fact remains that there is no statistical evidence that there is any difference between the sexes in terms of frequency or volume. It is true, however, that men do tend to be less discreet . . . and this we consider to be most reprehensible. Whilst **toilet-sounds** (as we shall call them) are nothing to be ashamed of, they are nothing to be proud of either. We totally disapprove of an 'honest vulgarity' that is becoming all too common these days whereby it is thought socially acceptable for people (usually men) to stand up at the dinner table or in a crowded bar, call for silence, and announce: 'Sh! Everybody! I'm going to fart!' Whereupon they raise one finger, one leg, and everybody else's eyebrows. We consider this sort of behaviour to be immodest, unnecessary and unpleasant. Nevertheless, we would say again, there is nothing shameful about making such noises; but the acceptable attitude must surely be **'everything in its place'**, and if the toilet isn't the appropriate place, then where is!?

However, nobody likes to be listened to. It is a dreadful moment to ask 'Where's the loo please?' and then be directed to a door no more than three feet from the dinner table; and it is extraordinary how a roomful of guests who have been bantering away happily at top volume will suddenly go dead silent the moment you have disappeared into the toilet. It is very difficult not to feel inhibited as you crouch there convinced that everyone is waiting with baited breath for you to break the silence. The slightest sound echoes round the bowl as if it were the Whispering Gallery at St Paul's. If there's no sound from the people outside you are convinced they've heard you, and are either suppressing their giggles or have all gone home in a state of shock. Worse still, it may seem to you that they are reacting to whatever noise you've just made . . . especially if it's followed by a gale of raucous laughter or even a cheer or a round of applause. Remember, this *could* be coincidence. Maybe they've got bored waiting for you to come out and have started playing charades. So don't be paranoid – they *may not* be listening to you. On the other hand . . . *they may*. Which is why this chapter is called **'covering the noise'**.

On entering the toilet **check round** to see if there are any **noise-making implements** or machines that can be turned on without arousing too much suspicion. A **radio** or **cassette-player** is of course the ultimate godsend. Try and choose a music station, and not 'talking', otherwise people might think you've got someone in there with you. Anyway, music 'covers' more efficiently – and the louder the better. You'll have to accept that it may be commented on if you've drowned out the after-dinner conversation but you can soon distract them by complimenting the host on his choice of audio equipment: 'Amazing power those little things have – I *must* get one.' Other welcome noise-makers are **extractor fans** – which, with any luck, will rattle like a single engine plane – **hairdryers** (usually kept in a little cupboard under the basin) and **electric shavers** (in the little cupboard *above* the basin). Always be ready with an explanation in case you're questioned. Using the extractor fan is self-explanatory and indeed desirable, though possibly the need for it may be taken as an indirect insult to the meal you've just had. As for the hairdryer and the shaver, it's not entirely loony to claim you felt you may as well groom yourself whilst you were in there, but **make sure the results show**. Give yourself a conspicuous quiff, and come out caressing your **newly shaved chin** (or if you're a lady, your newly-shaved **legs** or **armpits**). Don't use the shaver if you've got a beard, unless you come out without one.

If the weather is rough outside you may care to chance **opening the window** in the hope that the sound of a force-ten gale will drown any noises you may make. **Beware**, though, of what it might do to your hair – you might emerge looking as if you're wearing a fright-wig. And make sure it's not raining, or, if it is, drape yourself in a **bath towel** before sitting down. **Running taps** can make a noise like Niagara, which of course could be misinterpreted by anyone listening, but you may care to try them as a method of drowning toilet-sound. Your explanation of why you've had the tap on for four minutes could be: 'I was making sure the water heated up so I could wash my hands.' Make sure you *don't* wash your hands – you'll probably scald yourself.

There is one cardinal rule for any of the above methods: turn on whatever machine you're using (or open the window) **before you sit down** and get started and it's too late to be able to reach them without risking all sorts of mishaps.

You may of course consider it unacceptably stressful to have to explain away the row produced by a transistor radio, a blowdryer, an electric shaver, a force-ten gale and four running taps. You might prefer to take a risk on the whole process of 'number twos', hoping that just for once it might be silent. In which case, we wish you the very best of luck and admire your optimism. We would suggest though that you are **prepared** in case things do go wrong and any noises do slip out.

What you have to do is **blame something else**. In polite and public society it is of course customary to blame the **dog** for anything offensive detected round the dinner table. This doesn't work quite so well in the toilet. You *could* take a dog in with you, though you'd probably have to pretend to be blind in order to avert rigorous questioning. Mind you, the dog would no doubt bark so loudly at being locked up in there it would provide very effective 'cover'; but you'd be in trouble with the RSPCA. If it's a well-trained and docile dog it might even be quiet but you still couldn't really blame it for your inadvertent toilet-sounds as dogs are invariably silent when they do that sort of thing. So forget the dog.

There are in fact plenty of things in most toilets that you can blame for making the **rude noises** everyone has assumed were you. Scraping a **bathroom stool** on a rubber floor or lino is pretty effective (less effective on a deep-pile carpet). **Bathwater** running out can sound really revolting, especially if you put the plug halfway across the hole. And **inflatable plastic bath toys** can produce all manner of pseudo-flatulent effects if they're blown up, let down, squashed or rubbed. The thing is, of course, you don't have to actually *do* any of the things whilst you're in there, because you are hoping the operation is going to be silent and you won't need them . . . **but** if the worst does happen and you do emit toilet-sounds then you have your excuses ready. If, on your re-entry to the party, the guests are either staring straight at you, or avoiding your gaze, then it's a pretty safe bet they heard. You must then immediately come out with the 'true' explanation. The flaw with all these 'imitations' is of course that in order to be absolutely sure your bluff has worked, you'll have to 'demonstrate'. It is just possible that the assembled company may *not* have heard anything at all but now you have to draw attention to whatever is supposed to have gone on in there:

'Gosh, doesn't that stool make a funny noise if you accidently scrape it along the rubber floor, like I just did.' Or:

'Don't worry I pulled that plug out that somebody had accidently left half in.' Or you'll have to admit you've been playing with the baby's inflatable plastic Loch Ness Monster.

At all times try to be nonchalant and casual and the same is true if there are **no noise-making implements** available at all. In that case you may have to resort to **singing** (which requires surprisingly good breath control to do it simultaneously with the business you actually went in for) or if you feel a toilet-sound coming on you can feign a violent coughing or sneezing fit. Whatever you do, though, **don't overdo it** as it will *attract* attention as much as distract, and if you have not developed your skills in covering the noise to a sufficient degree of subtlety and confidence it may be all too obvious that you have something to hide . . . but it's always worth a try. Finally, don't **blush** – and don't do it again at the dinner table.

No paper

Some of the most common and potentially uncomfortable 'toilet problems' are caused by **lack of toilet paper**. We're sure many of us have experienced the distress of having to 'drip-dry' due to the shortcomings of careless or unobservant toilet-owners. Owners and users alike take note.

There are many types of toilet paper. They range from the *ultra-soft*, which is usually found wrapped around scampering puppies, to the *ultra-hard* which, when not rolled and perforated, could easily be found wrapped around parcels. Just one layer will ensure safe delivery. This particular type usually smells like rancid disinfectant and has the absorption of baco-foil. It doesn't feel dissimilar. Its one (and only?) advantage is that it doesn't cost very much (neither does wire wool but that doesn't mean we have to use it in the toilet). If this is the type you find you are lacking (you can usually tell by the white porcelain letter-box by the side of the WC) then you are **better off without it**. Although you can make the unpleasant commodity slightly less so by **crinkling** it up before use (see page 31 – 'Origami').

Now, if you are in the privacy of your own home and you discover the dreaded **empty toilet-roll holder** you can, if there are other members of your family around, **shout** out for someone to **throw** you in a toilet roll. Alternatively, if you are alone, you can easily **waddle off** with your trousers round your ankles and find some for yourself. However, if you are at someone else's house and trying to make a reasonably good impression, these methods are not to be recommended.

After spending a few hours at a sophisticated cocktail or dinner party ingratiating yourself to whatever members of whichever is your opposite sex and being heralded by all and sundry as the mysterious, smooth-talking wit of the evening, the last thing you want to do is excuse yourself softly and swagger into the WC, only to swagger out again and ask the elegant hostess for a toilet roll.

At best no one but the hostess will hear. At worst, *everyone but* the hostess will hear and you will have to repeat the embarrassing request. The hostess, cigarette in one hand, whisky sour in the other, will then glide off to find the aforementioned article while you smile weakly at the assembled throng and shift from one foot to the other until she reappears and hands you the single, drooping white roll. You will then thank her kindly and slither back into the WC, roll in hand.

Worse still, and almost unthinkable, you could discover the shortcoming **after** already having committed yourself to a healthy bout of '**number twos**'.

If you want to retain any credibility at all for the rest of the evening, on **no account** shout through the room: 'Can someone throw me a toilet roll!' and it goes without saying that **waddling** out with one's trousers round one's ankles is, even for the most disturbingly exhibitionist amongst us, a very **bad** idea.

If the gathering is large, ie. a wedding or christening, you may be able to do the following: open the door very slightly and try and attract the attention of a **small child**. When you have, explain your predicament and offer them some **trinket** or **boiled sweet** in return for a toilet roll.

If you find you have neither sweet nor trinket you may find the young person quite content with the offer of your **watch**, signet **ring** or any family **heirloom** you may have about you and feel prepared to part with at the time. Be warned though, your brain is befuddled by the desperation of your plight and, in retrospect, thoughts of how your great-grandfather would have reacted had he known that his most treasured and coveted solid gold fob-watch had been handed over to a drooling four-year-old in return for a toilet roll might well keep you awake for a few nights afterwards. Better to make absolutely certain that you have a bag of assorted **sweets** or a small selection of **bendy toys** with you when you go out. This little piece of forethought could prove as invaluable as your great-grandfather's fob-watch. However the scheme is not infallible.

If you are lucky the child will scamper off downstairs, fetch the required article, and with no fuss nor bother at all hand it **discreetly** through the door in return for its reward. If you are unlucky, the child will skip downstairs to the roomful of people and shout over at its mother:

'Mummy – Mr Morris has done poo-poos and there's no botty wipes!'

This is the stuff of nightmares, but it could all so easily be avoided. The **first** thing you do on entering an unfamiliar toilet is **check** if there is any paper. If there is not only **no paper** but . . . the **cardboard bit in the centre** has also been used, **don't panic**. Look around. Can you see a pouting **plastic doll** in a crocheted crinoline? Can you see a knitted white **poodle** with a distended stomach? Can you see a **macramé wart-hog**?

One would hope that one or other of these distasteful articles would conceal the **spare roll**. If they don't, there's possibly something mentally wrong with your host. It is a very odd phenomenon, but on the whole, people are quite willing to display the toilet roll that is in use but slightly less enthusiastic about revealing the spare. Personally, we would rather see a toilet roll than a macramé wart-hog.

Be that as it may.

One thing that is very important and **must** be remembered is that if after a frantic search you do unearth the spare roll, **stay calm**. There have been countless occasions when the toilet-goer has been so *excited* by his or her find that they have accidently and almost immediately **dropped** it **down the toilet**. This is an extremely nasty moment especially if you have just **'been'**. Not only do you still have nothing with which to wipe yourself but you now have the problem of a **sodden** and rapidly **expanding** toilet roll.

For the sake of your own dignity you must **get rid** of this swollen reminder of what might have been as quickly as possible.

You can do one of these three things:

a throw it in the **bin** and cover it up with something
b shove it at the bottom of the **loo-brush holder**
c throw it out of the **window**

If none of these are possible, **wedge** it in the S-bend at the back of the toilet and hope to God that by the time your hosts find it you will be long gone.

(This accident can also occur when the inexperienced toilet-goer tries to fit a toilet roll onto an unfamiliar holder. Some are easy and straightforward. Some require a degree in mechanical engineering to master. One inadvertent flick of the wrist and it's in the pan. Take our advice: **leave** the roll on the floor, and the complex task to your host or hostess.)

So, you are **still** without toilet paper. You have exhausted all the possibilities, and yourself.

There is **no** current or spare roll.

There is **no cardboard** bit in the middle.

But there is still **hope**.

Look around. . . .

Can you see a **towel? A flannel? A furry cover on the loo seat?** A pair of **curtains? A bath mat? A cat?** To the desperate these may seem like a good idea but please on **no account** be tempted. Just think how you would feel if someone used **your** curtains, towel, furry cover, flannel, bathmat . . . or cat!

But can you see a **pot plant?** The odd **leaf** or two would certainly not go amiss. Lift up the **carpet**: the floorboards may be lined with a veritable trove of old newspapers. Sift through the **rubbish bin**: can you see a jar of your hostess's **cotton wool balls?** A dried-up **J-cloth?** Go through your pockets: you may find all manner of old sweet wrappers and cigarette packets. You may also find a wallet full of **five-pound notes**. Now these would be the answer – soft and absorbent but, alas, very costly. If you think it's worth it, and you can afford it, go ahead, but if you have any misgivings at all – an unpaid gas bill, a starving child or an overdue Equity subscription – put all such thoughts out of your head immediately. Instead . . . is there a window? If there is, open it and look outside. There may well be a **tree** close by yielding handfuls of large leaves. The very thing! Use them and you can re-enter the dining room with your reputation and wallet full of five-pound notes completely intact.

Nevertheless, the fact remains that if you had left your house prepared this never would have happened. **Before** you leave to go anywhere *check* that you have a pocketful of tissues, and a bag full of boiled sweets and a selection of bendy toys. Never go anywhere without them.

But for the moment, if all else has failed turn to page 97.

Well . . . hopefully you have nearly finished . . . but not quite . . . there is still the . . .

Flushing

You have nearly completed what would appear to be a totally successful toilet operation, having overcome the absence of lock, seat and paper, and drowned out any undesirable sounds. You have repelled intruders by keeping the door jammed with your walking-stick; you maintained a perfect balance by holding on to the towel rail; you used a 1947 copy of the *Daily Sketch* that you discovered under the wobbly leg of an antique commode; and you've also managed three immaculately synchronized coughs. Feeling relieved and rather proud you are ready to rejoin the dinner party, suppressing a strong urge to burst out of the toilet punching the air in triumph and yelling: 'I did it!' Mind you, you would be justified – you have achieved so much and surely vanquished 'the terror of the toilet'?! But no. It still has one final cruel trick to play on you. It **won't flush**. Isn't life unfair?

You can of course decide to come straight out with it, march into the dining room and **announce** to one and all:

'The toilet won't flush.'

'Oh . . . have you er . . . done "anything"?'

'Yes. **Everything**. And it's still there.'

It's not really the sort of thing guests want to hear just as they are about to eat – nor indeed **whilst** they are eating – and definitely **not** just **after** they've eaten. Besides it's likely that your humiliation will get immediately worse. Either the host or hostess's small child will rush in and flush it first go – in which case you feel a bit of a pranny – or the host and hostess and half the guests will surge into the toilet to try and sort it out, thereby witnessing the extent of the problem – in which case you feel faintly 'unclean'.

We shall assume that you would rather, if at all possible, **do it yourself**.

Take your time and try and think logically. **Why** won't it flush? Because there is **no chain?** This could be because it is a new fangled push-button toilet. So take a moment for a brief search – the button could be on top, covered by an old copy of **Country Life**, or it could be on the floor, under the bathroom scales. Or there might be a little handle on the side of the cistern. If you can find any of these, your troubles are over – unless of course they don't work. In which case, it *still* won't flush. And it won't flush if you get over-excited and snap the handle off; or yank too hard on the piece of string that dangles where the chain used to be and it *comes away* in **your hand**.

Let's assume there is **no chain** (and no button either) . . . maybe the previous toilet-goer pulled it off and it fell in the pan and disappeared round the S-bend and they were too embarrassed to let anyone know. You must now **climb up** on the toilet to reach the cistern. Be careful neither to slip and put your foot down the loo, nor to capsize the whole pedestal. You may help your balance by resting one hand on the cistern, but don't hang on to it or you'll pull it down on your head. If there is a hanging light don't hang on to that either, as you'll probably electrocute yourself, and if you've got one foot down the pan it could be fatal. Try and **spread-eagle yourself** so that some pressure is taken by the toilet walls, rather in the manner of Spiderman. With one hand, **raise the cistern lid** – do not trap your fingers, nor let the lid fall off and crush your foot. Now reach inside and **feel for the ball-cock**. Be warned that a ball-cock feels almost as obscene as it sounds, and if you've never felt one before, especially when it's ice-cold and covered in slime, you may yelp. Don't.

Now gently **press down** on the ball-cock and with luck the toilet will flush. Without luck, the 'ball' will **snap off** the '**cock**', and the cistern will overflow and continue to do so, drenching yourself and ruining the toilet walls and floor, and the ceiling of the apartment below. You must decide for yourself whether or not you wish to take this risk. You may be better advised to always carry a **spare chain** – the better quality ones can be worn round the neck threaded through a medallion.

Unfortunately, the spare chain is not always the solution since there are toilets with chains, or buttons or handles that will **still not flush**. Before attempting the ball-cock method consider the possibility that a **'special routine'** may be necessary. A considerate host will have advised you of this before you went in: '. . . hold it down for ten seconds, then let it go and then do it again, quickly.' You know the sort of thing. If they've said nothing, you'll have to work it out for yourself. Admittedly it's a bit like trying to guess the combination of a safe but it's worth trying a few of the more obvious moves before admitting defeat. The following have worked for us. . . .

'One short quick hard pull' – a sprained wrist is usually an indication that you're doing it right.

'One long pull . . . hold it, count seven and then let go.'

'Three and a half short pulls in quick succession . . .'

Whatever you do . . . don't pump it. Give the cistern time to recover after each unsuccessful attempt. Toilets are like cars: the more you try to get them going, the less likely they are to start at all – it's the equivalent of flooding the carburettor or flattening the battery, only the failure is rather messier.

If everything so far has failed you can often flush a stubborn toilet by pouring a **large bucket of water** down it. Very few toilets are equipped with a large bucket, and some of them don't even have a tap in them. We do **not** suggest you always carry a large bucket, unless you're prepared to pose as a window cleaner. (Which is not *that* bad an idea, as window cleaners are often considered to be very good value at parties since they have such a fund of funny stories . . . but if you're not *really* a window cleaner you might be a bit of a disappointment to expectant guests.) If there is no bucket, you may well find a **large waste-paper bin** in a bathroom, or a **laundry basket**, and so you could fill one of these with water. Do make sure though that it is not the perforated kind – straw and wickerwork are **not** water retentive.

There might well be a **potty** (especially if there are small kids in the house) in which case fill it up and **pour it down**, and the toilet **may well flush**. On the other hand, it still may not. In this unhappy and unpleasant event the least you can do is leave it as concealed and as fragrant as possible. Fill the bowl to the brim with toilet paper (if there is any) and pour in any disinfectant that may be hidden behind the pipes. If there is no disinfectant, raid the bathroom cabinet for anything that smells nice – aftershave or French perfume – and pour it down the loo. The aroma will be surprisingly pleasant. You may care to enhance the effect by shaping the pieces of toilet paper into **imitation roses** (see page 29 – 'Origami'). The pedestal will look and smell like a large Grecian urn full of flowers, and the host and hostess will be so taken with it that they are unlikely to disturb the display for several days by which time they'll have forgotten who was responsible or why.

The unflushable toilet is indeed a most unsavoury and unnerving experience but for sheer unparalleled horror it cannot compare with the exact opposite – the **toilet** that **won't stop**.

This is the result of a blocked S-bend – maybe the previous toilet-goer dropped the spare roll down there. There is no way you could know, and nothing you can do. Your satisfaction at flushing it first time turns to blind terror as the water rises higher and higher towards the lip of the bowl, threatening to drown the room, yourself and the world in an unspeakable flood of . . .

We have **no advice to give**. All you can do is slam the lid down, sit on it, and **pray**. . . .

If your prayers are answered the waters will subside.

But it's not over yet.

Personal appearance in and out of the toilet

(This section particularly applies to the ladies.)

I think we can safely say that the moment women fear most in their lives is the one when they discover that, after a visit to the toilet, they have just walked the entire length of a busy restaurant with their **dress tucked in their knickers**.

The peculiar thing is that witnesses of this revealing predicament very rarely mention it to the person concerned. This leaves the unfortunate woman striding purposefully and confidently through an endless valley of chattering, clattering tables full of people, blissfully unaware of the pointing fingers, jutting elbows, silent smirks and sniggers she is leaving in her wake. And IT'S NOT JUST THE CUSTOMERS.

Don't kid yourself. Restaurant staff will kill for this moment. The slimy, patronising maître-d' that has just spent ten minutes fawning all over your ash tray can now be found scampering into the smoke-filled kitchen and informing the **slavering herd of Spanish kitchen staff** of the sighting. Most of whom haven't seen a pair of knickers since Mama bent down in the garlic patch.

By the time the wretched woman has reached her table and bemused escort, she'll have a crowd milling around behind her resembling the audience of a Saturday-night nude mud-wrestling contest.

Let's face it, we all take proper care and attention of our appearance when we know 'certain regions' will be on show but when accidents like this occur how can you possibly always be prepared? It could be one of those nights, when, for one reason or another, you just didn't bother. You could be wearing anything from crotchless leopard-skin thermals to an old pair of ex-spouse's Y-fronts.

We cannot stress how important it is to **check yourself** before you leave the WC. This sort of thing isn't always going to happen to someone else . . . one day **it could be you** . . . and it could be even worse.

Ladies have also been known to leave a toilet with one end of a seemingly **endless roll** of toilet paper **tucked in** somewhere under their voluminous petticoats. (Presumably in their crotchless, leopard-skin thermals!)

This **appalling incident** once happened to a lady mayoress friend of ours. The poor lady had almost walked halfway along a line of curtseying Conservative Women's Guild members before her husband, who was striding up behind her, noticed the peculiar, umbilical-like growth stretching from his wife's nether regions to the open 'Guild Hall' door.

The quick-thinking gentleman swiftly bobbed down like a bunny girl, sliced through the stream of two-ply with the ceremonial scissors and smiled broadly at the row of bewildered, conservative ladies. The crowd in turn applauded and nothing more was said of the potentially even more embarrassing incident. The lady mayoress never even knew!

But no matter how prepared you are for the inevitability of incidents such as these, a bit of assistance in that direction from WC owners would definitely not go amiss.

The thoughtful addition of a mirror on the wall will tell you that you are spruce at a glance but have you noticed how many WCs do **not** have a **mirror on the wall**? They may have magazines, posters, collages or mobiles so why not a mirror? How else are you supposed to know if you have a piece of spinach between your teeth, custard in your beard or a glutinous bogey hanging out of your nose? Admittedly there may be a mirror in the hall or dining-room but who wants to stand in front of a roomful of people picking one's nose?

Considering that most social gatherings rely almost solely on face-to-face encounters we find the omission of a looking-glass in a WC totally irresponsible if not downright suspicious. Do you not think that it might be to the host or hostess's advantage that *they* are managing to remain pristine throughout the evening, due to inside knowledge of the whereabouts of a mirror, whilst their hapless guests are laughing and chatting away to one another, totally unaware that they are rapidly turning into something out of the 'THRILLER' video.

Watch out for these **signs**:

a Has your conversational partner suddenly **changed the subject** to nasal passages or **green slimy things**?
b Does he or she keep looking down his or her nose?
c Does he or she keep looking down *your* nose?
d Every time you smile at them do people wince and throw up?

If you are aware of any of these tell-tale signs get into that WC **ASAP** – OK?

Reflection ruses

We have already established that there is **no mirror** in this pathetically clad toilet. Do not be daunted. Try looking into **the taps**. If they are well kept and shiny you may be able to spot any undesirable appendage you may have acquired reflected in the recesses of their undulating stainless steel. Beware though – they may also give you the appearance of the Elephant Man! (Which may come as no surprise if you *are* the Elephant Man; and is otherwise small enough price to pay for 'spotting the spinach'.)

If the taps are too cloudy and grubby (which wouldn't surprise us judging from the state of this toilet so far) try looking at your reflection in a brass door knob, the small square window-pane, or the metal flushing handle.

If you still have no luck rush back to the dining table and pick up a **knife**. Hold the knife up to your face and look at your reflection. Check your nose, then **bare your teeth**: only please be careful not to be spotted. The sight of you leering into your razor-sharp steak knife could easily be misconstrued. (Get a friend to try it and you'll see what we mean. In fact stainless-steel meat cleavers make even better teeth-reflectors, but don't risk them. People have been shot for looking less suspicious.)

Of course, as ever, all this rushing backwards and forwards could have been avoided with a **little forethought**.

A small round **looking-glass** concealed in a tissue can be gazed into at any point during the evening merely on the pretence of blowing your nose. (If you *do* blow your nose, don't forget to remove the glass.) Or you can pretend you have something in your eye, and while you are busy blinking and poking away at the bloodshot eyeball do a quick tour of any other orifices in the vicinity. It you notice something amiss, slip into the WC, take a jolly good look, have a thorough pick, and, while you're at it, check skirts, knickers, and toilet paper are still at a safe distance from one another. Since you've got your mirror you may as well practise your ventriloquial exercises and wiggle your ears (see page 14) before leaving the smallest room calm, confident and ready to be the life and soul of the party.

Unless, of course, you suffer from . . .

Leaking

This is, we believe, an exclusively masculine problem and so we are now addressing you men. A lot of blokes suffer from **delayed drip**. You know the problem: no matter how much you shake or squeeze it, a few little spare drops seep out just after you've put it away. If it happens to you . . . read on. Do not feel lonely or ashamed. It is *not* a sign of imminent incontinence or a reversion to bed-wetting. Look round any company of men and you can bet a high percentage of them will be delayed drippers: but you won't always be able to spot them by that tell-tale little **damp patch**, simply because **they** have learnt to fold half a dozen pieces of toilet paper into an absorbent **pad** and stuffed it down their underpants – and you thought they were just well endowed didn't you?

Well, now that you know the truth, that's two paranoias you've overcome. You are probably no 'smaller' than the next man; and he too is probably a delayed dripper. If, however, you have been over-confident and neglectful and **forgotten** your little **pad** then there are few things more humilitating than emerging from the toilet with a visible 'dark area' between your legs.

There is only one way to disguise it, and that is by rendering the rest of your trousers the same colour so that it will **blend in**. You can do this before you leave the loo by filling the toothbrush mug with water and **pouring it over yourself**. If there is no mug, fill the wash basin, take off your trousers, and dunk them. If there is no wash basin, you may have to flush the toilet and use the clean water from the pan. In any event it is unlikely that the effect will be entirely uniform, but at least the dark areas will be widespread and less specific. On re-entering the room you should **blame the tap** (if there was one):

'There must have been an airlock – the water suddenly spurted out and soaked me!'

If there was no tap in the toilet you have little choice but to try and soak your trousers thoroughly to an even shade, put them back on and hope on one will notice they are wringing wet. **Try not to wince** when you sit down.

Alternatively, you may prefer to soak yourself the minute you come out before anyone has had time to register your dilemma – but do it quickly.

Try knocking your drink into your lap as you're squeezing back into your chair. Wine is less painful than hot coffee. If you are an habitual dripper you may not feel entirely confident or happy about resorting to any of these admittedly uncomfortable solutions; nor perhaps are you prepared to stuff thick wads of padding down your pants in case the resulting bulge raises expectations in the opposite sex which may later not be fulfilled. In which case you could **pretend** to be **Scottish**. Highland traditional dress seems to be ideal for covering the embarrassment of a 'delayed dripper'. It is unlikely that a free-flowing **kilt** will be noticeably moistened at all and, even if it is, the resulting damp patch will be efficiently and completely masked by a **dangling sporran**. Come to think of it, under your kilt, you could wear a pair of **tartan Y-fronts**, stuffed with drip-retentive *sponge* or a strategically positioned empty milk *bottle*, and no one would be the wiser.

Fig. 16.

THE UNPREPARED TOILET-GOER

The Complete Toilet-Goer

During the preceding pages we have suggested a variety of items that you should always carry with you when you intend to visit another person's toilet.

There were quite a lot of them, and it strikes us that you might appreciate a simple checklist that you can tick off before leaving the house.

So . . . **never** forget the following:

In case there's no lock on the door: a strong, crooked walking-stick (can be concealed down a trouser leg); a wedge; and a length of rope (can be worn round the waist under loose clothing, or over the shoulder if impersonating a mountaineer)

To cope with rough, cracked or loose seats: a pair of tweezers (for removing splinters); a small piece of sandpaper, a tube of polyfilla and an adjustable monkey wrench

To cover toilet-sounds: a pocket-sized transistor radio, or a dog

In case there's no paper: a box of tissues; or a bag of boiled sweets and a selection of bendy toys (for bribing children). A daily paper

In case the loo won't flush: a spare chain (can be worn round the neck, with or without a pendant) and a large bucket (if impersonating a window-cleaner)

Ladies and gentlemen: a small round looking-glass

Men only: an empty milk bottle, a sporran and a kilt

N.B. It is, in our opinion, by no means unacceptable that a man could be a Scottish window-cleaner whose hobby is mountain climbing.

Fig. 17.

THE COMPLETE TOILET-GOER

1. Rope (also useful for securing yourself against turbulence in plane or boat loos)
2. Spare chain
3. Sandpaper
4. Newspaper (for emergency use)
5. Polyfilla
6. Sporran
7. Crooked walking-stick
8. Kilt
9. Bendy toys & boiled sweets
10. Monkey wrench
11. Dog not shown (unless it's in here)
12. (Under kilt) absorbent sponge
13. (Under kilt) truss for securing milk bottle
14. Bucket & window-cleaner's leather (useful for wiping up continental toilets)
15. Transistor radio
16. Empty milk bottle

Appendix I: Euphemisms

If you wish to use someone else's toilet it is important to make your request clear and unambiguous. Personally, we suggest you say in a loud, confident and unembarrassed voice: 'Please, I want to use the toilet.'

Unfortunately many people are so inhibited they find such frankness impossible. They resort to euphemisms. If, as a host or hostess, you are faced with an oblique and mystifying request then you should always assume that whoever is talking to you wants to go to the lavatory. Now and again they might be equally mystified if you direct them to the loo when they were actually asking if you knew anything about micro-computers, but they won't be offended (they're bound to need it some time anyway) and nine times out of ten you'll have done the right thing. What *is* embarrassing for a potential toilet-goer is if your ignorance of his or her anxious euphemisms forces them to express their need in more vulgar terms. If after five minutes of unintelligible exchange they suddenly scream!

'Christ! I'm dying for a crap!' then you can be sure you've been obtuse.

Therefore, please read and absorb the following expressions and learn to recognise them even if they are delivered in a soft or shaky voice. . . .

We assume the vulgar terms are all too well-known and since they are what we are trying to avoid saying we have no intention of using them here. We imagine the groupings that follow make the meanings obvious enough.

'Please, where is . . .'

The little boys' room. The little girls' room. The comfort station. The john. The smallest room. The loo. The WC or Water Closet.

The powder room. The bog. The Ladies. The Gents. 'It'. The Khazi. The can.

'I need to . . .'

Do a tinkle. Point Percy at the porcelain. Have a leak. Do number ones. Turn my bike over. Have a slash. Wee wee. Relieve myself. Have a jimmy riddle. Strain the greens. Powder my nose. Do little jobs. Have a widdle. Spend a penny. Syphon the Python. Douse the duke.

'I may even need to. . .'

Do number twos. Do big jobs. Do big ones. Powder my nose again. Do plops plops. Go for a pony and trap. Do ukky poos.

'Whoops, sorry, I've just. . .'

Broken wind. Pooped. Blown off. Let one go. Done a raspberry tart. Trumped. Dropped one. Let off. Done a botty burp.

Now add your own. . . .

(For Emergency Use Only)